KES TWO ONE

BEHIND CLOSED DOORS

BEHIND CLOSED DOORS

A MARRIAGE MANUAL WITH NEARLY 2000 PHOTOGRAPHS

PHOTOGRAPHS BY ROBIN SCHWARTZ
INTRODUCTION BY DRS. PHYLLIS AND EBERHARD KRONHAUSEN
DESIGNED BY HERB LUBALIN

MATERIA MEDICA, PUBLISHERS OF MEDICAL TEXTS
251 WEST 57TH STREET, NEW YORK, N.Y. 10019

TITLE LETTERING: TONY DISPIGNA
DESIGN ASSEMBLAGE: ELIZABETH GRIFFITHS
COPY EDITING: SHOSHANA GINZBURG
PROOFREADING: SUSAN ROGERS
DISPLAY TYPEFACE: SERIF GOTHIC
TEXT TYPEFACE: AVANT-GARDE GOTHIC
PHOTOGRAPHIC DARKROOM: MODERN AGE LABS

ABOUT THE PHOTOGRAPHER AND MODELS

Robin Schwartz, who took the photographs for this book, enjoys international renown that is surprising for one so young: She is only in her early twenties. She has shot photographs for major magazines, been exhibited in museums on three continents, been published in books, has worked on feature films, and created her own film documentaries. The models who posed for her in this book are friends of hers, in London where all three reside. The models are a husband-wife pair of dancers originally from Paris named Gisele and Pierre. Lucky Pierre!

INTRODUCTION

BY DRS. PHYLLIS C. AND EBERHARD W. KRONHAUSEN

We have been psychologists and sexual counselors all of our professional lives, but NEVER, in over twenty years, have we come across a set of erotic photographs as lyrical, sexy, instructive and potentially helpful as those in this book. They show an uncommonly attractive young couple in wildly abandoned acts of lovemaking. The photographs are explicit—as sex-educational pictures ought to be; clear, unambiguous representations of human sexual activity. Robin Schwartz's camera never blinks, and her photography is artistic, masterful. She never coyly spins her lens out of focus at the critical moment; she never cops out, as do so many other photographers of the erotic.

Yet the photographs in "Behind Closed Doors," for all their frankness, are never crude or vulgar. They scrupulously maintain highest standards of good taste, even when dealing with the most intimate aspects of lovemaking.

The married couple shown in the nearly 2,000 pictures in this book no doubt helped move the photographer to create this masterpiece. Their consuming love for each other radiates from each frame and surely inspired the photographer. The pictures show not only bodies joining but spirits and minds, not only thrilling relations but a thrilling relationSHIP. Here sex has become a means of total communication between two sensitive individuals—a phenomenon as rare in the fantasy world of erotic photography as in real life. Gisele and Pierre are so uninhibited and joyous in their lovemaking that the reader does not feel like an "intruder." The couple is completely un-selfconscious and the reader simply follows the pair from room to room in their big old house, fascinated by their imaginative sex capers. Then, too, there is an unspoken invitation. One senses that these two people mean to have the reader share their sensual delight, vicariously. By the time you finish the book, you feel you've known Gisele and Pierre all your life.

From a sex counselor's point of view, these photos are important for still another reason: Not only is this couple beautifully uninhibited and enthusiastic in their lovemaking; they are also unusually inventive. They relish and ravish each other in every conceivable manner, in every part of the house—on the dining room table, kitchen counter, chessboard, shower floor, even stairway. One is almost surprised when, at last, one finds them making love—in bed! How many couples—even newlyweds—are even half as inspired and resourceful in their lovemaking? How many times have we, as psychologists and sex counselors, heard the complaints of couples about sexual boredom and loss of interest in sexual activity even on the part of recently married couples? For all such couples this picture book can be a treasure and guide, a source of invaluable therapeutic help. The fact that these pictures demonstrate an amazing variety of positions without the slightest hint of "perversion," "kinkiness," or "deviation" makes the book even more unusual.

In short, this is the CONSUMMATE pictorial sex manual. It is art, education, and turn-on—all at once. We hope that millions of couples throughout the world, no matter what their language, will be able to benefit from these delightful and informative pictures which, without need for a single word of explanation or caption, provide a complete sex education. "Behind Closed Doors" is truly visual sex education at its scintillating best.

1: PORTAL TO PLEASURE

II: MAKING IT UP THE STAIRS

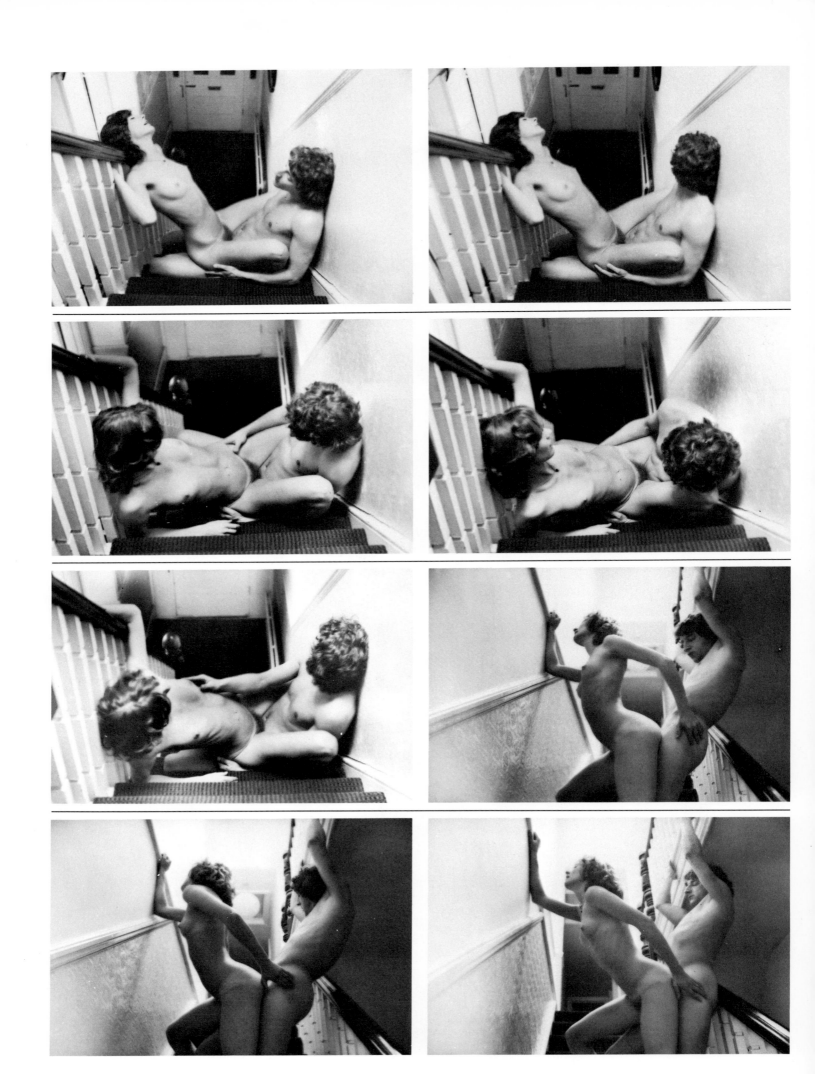

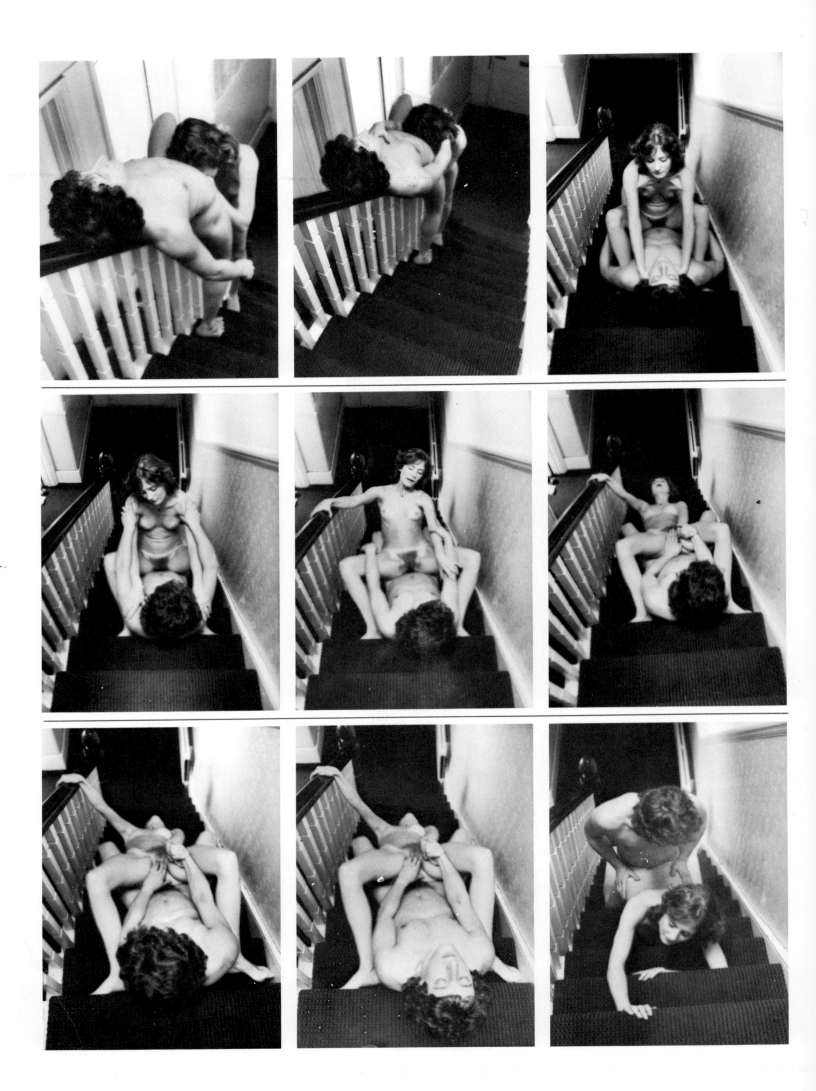

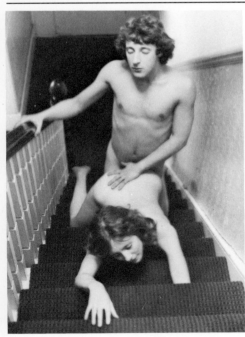  

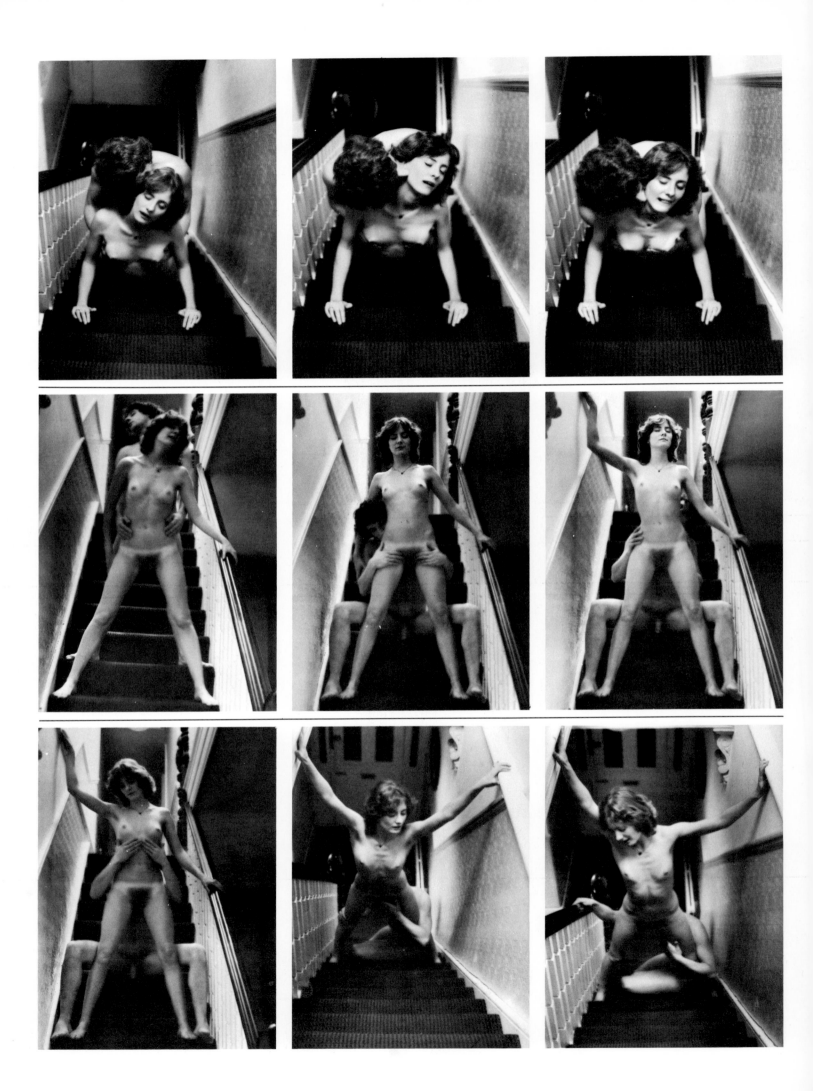

III: LOITERING IN THE HALL

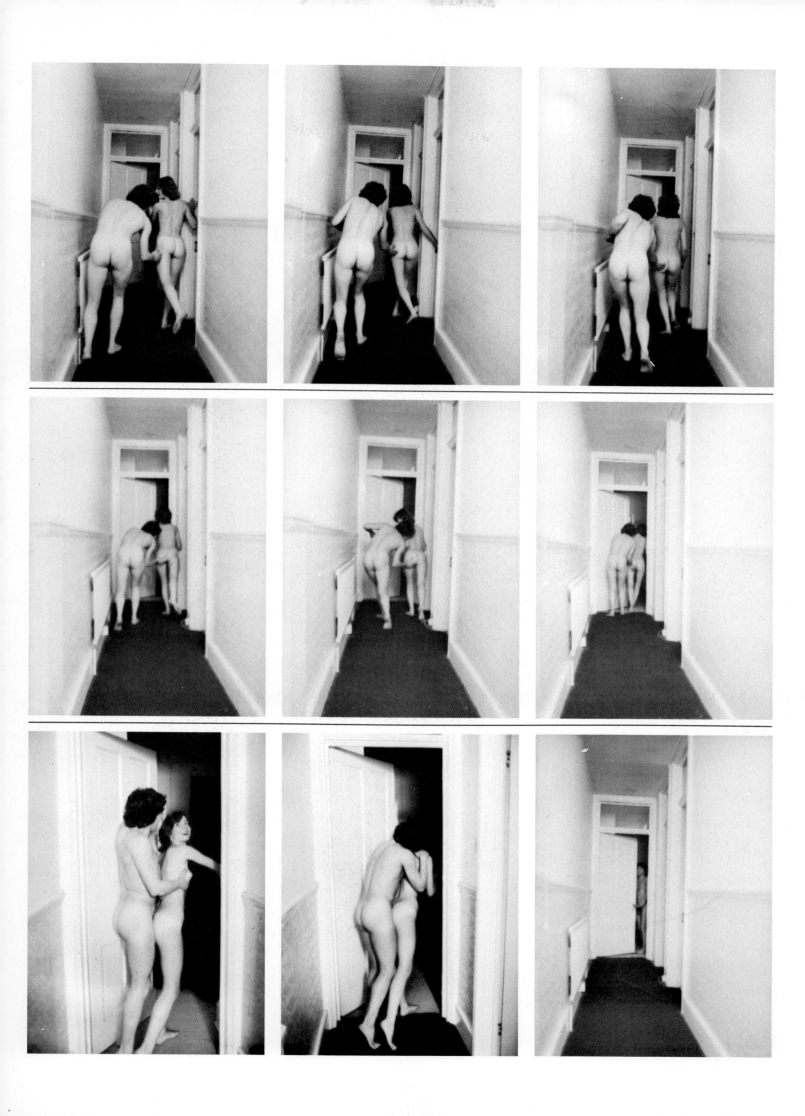

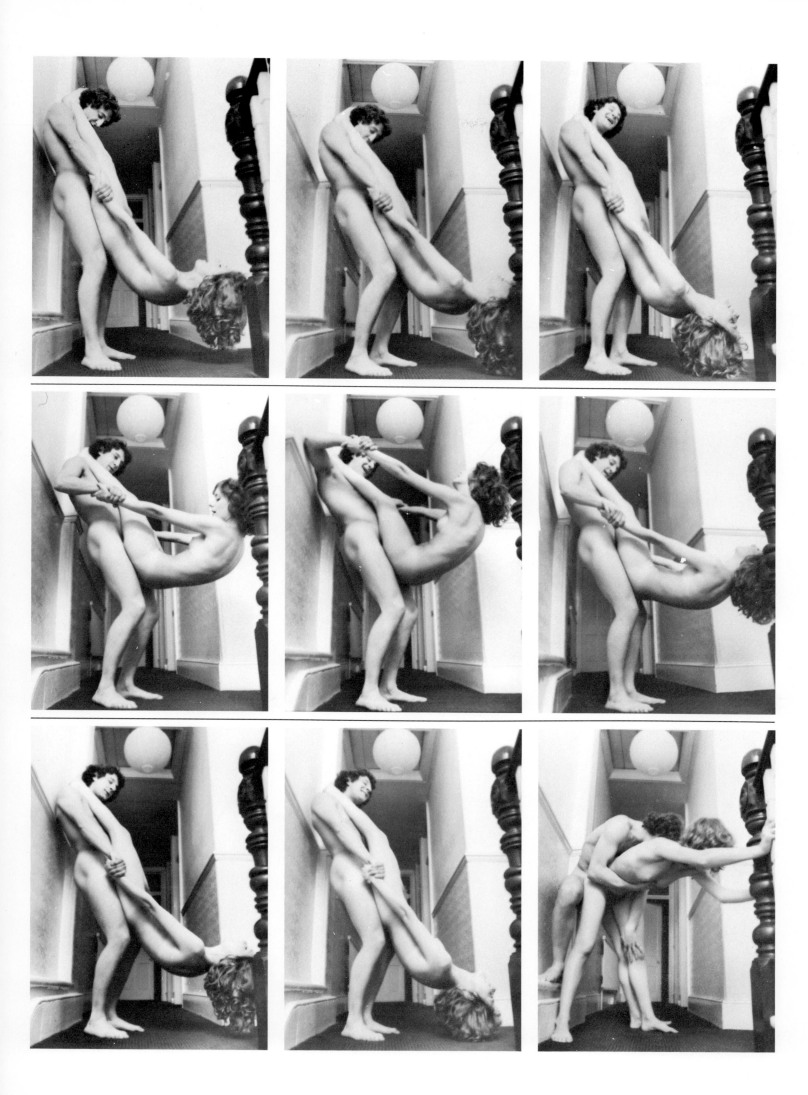

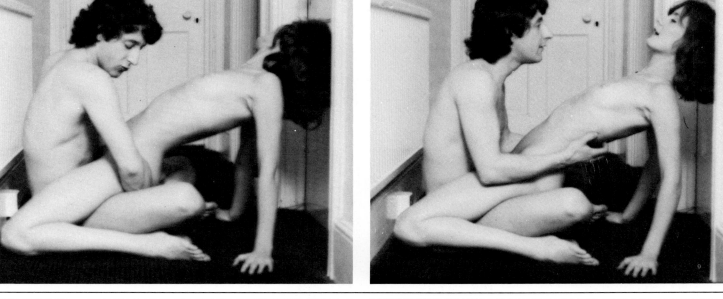

IV: COOKING IN THE KITCHEN

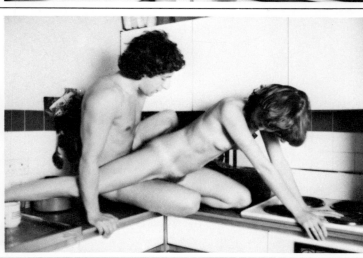

V: INSATIABLE APPETITES

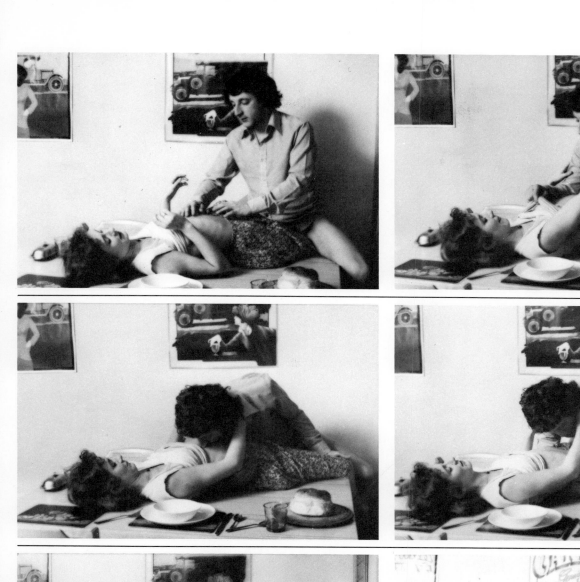

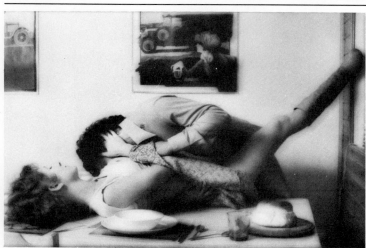
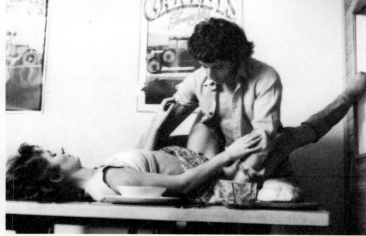

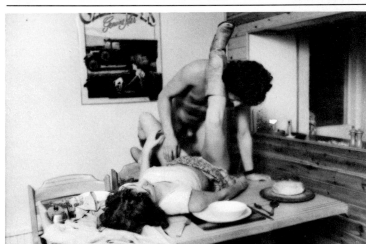

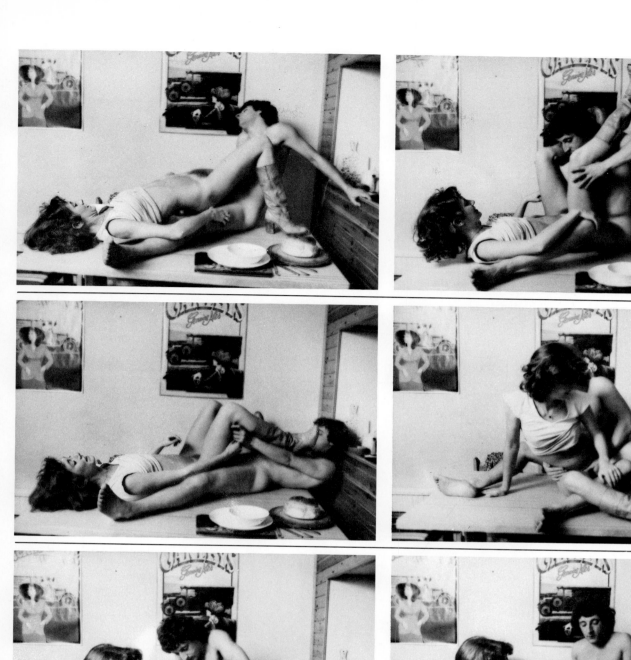

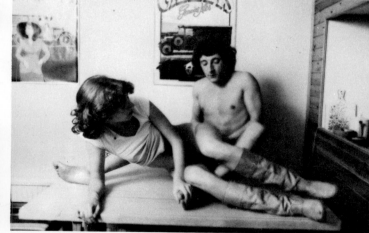

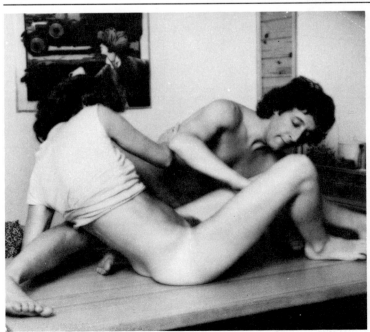

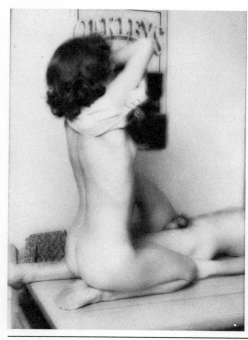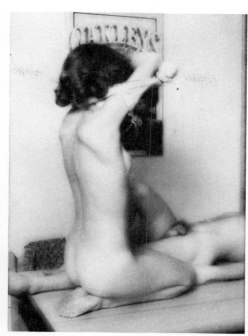

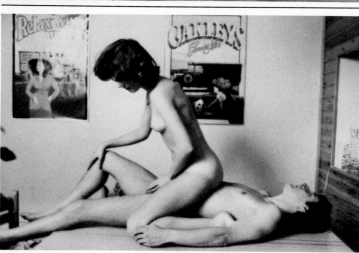

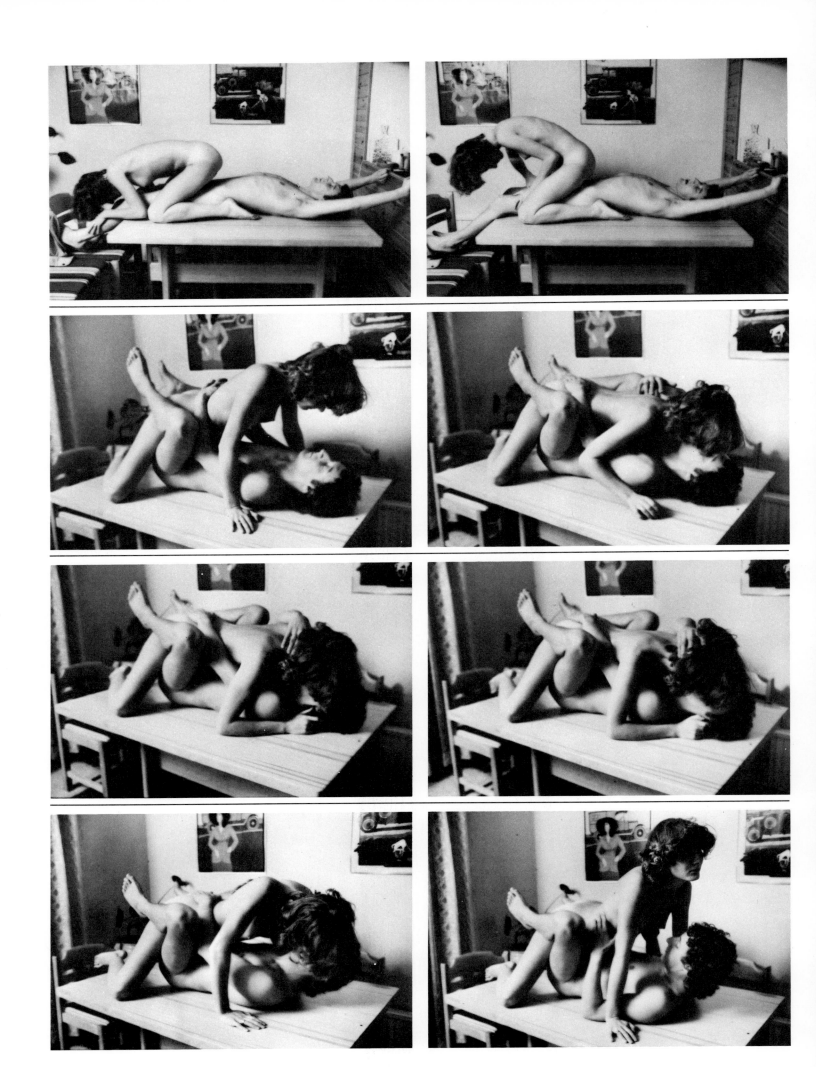

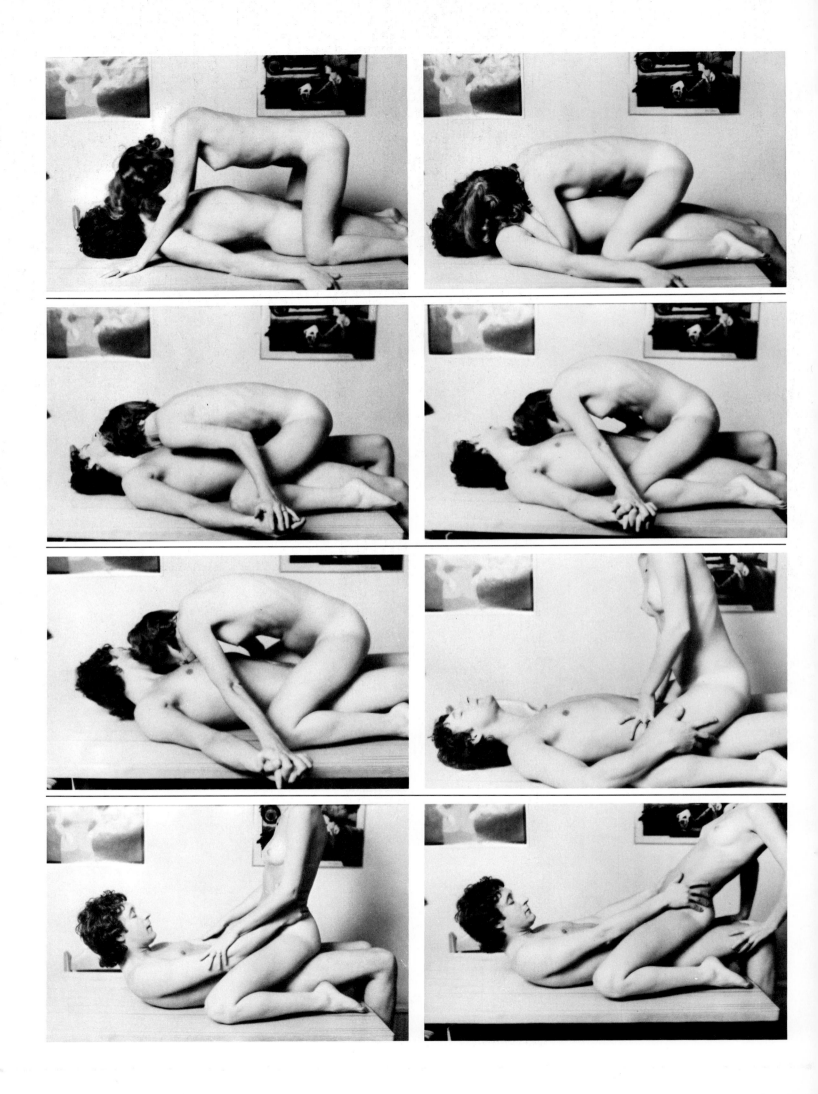

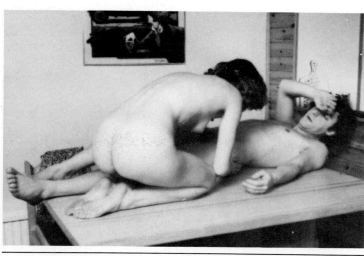

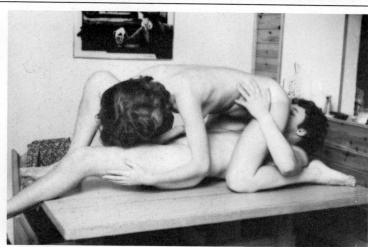

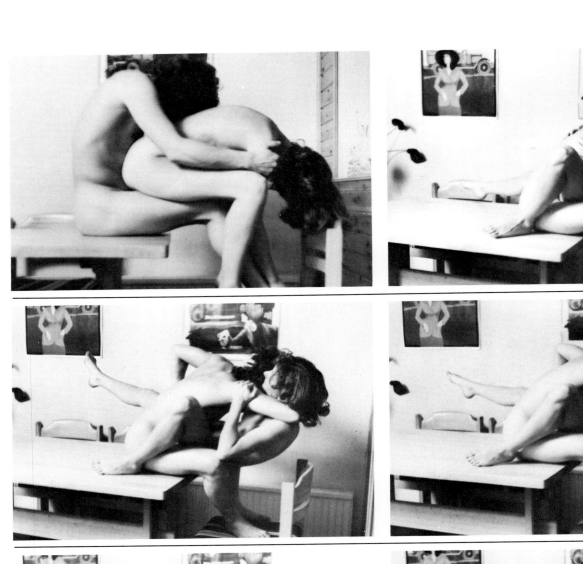

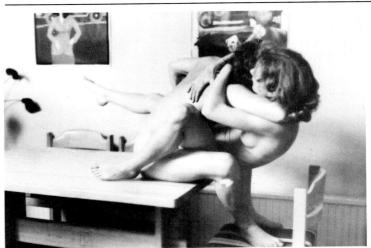

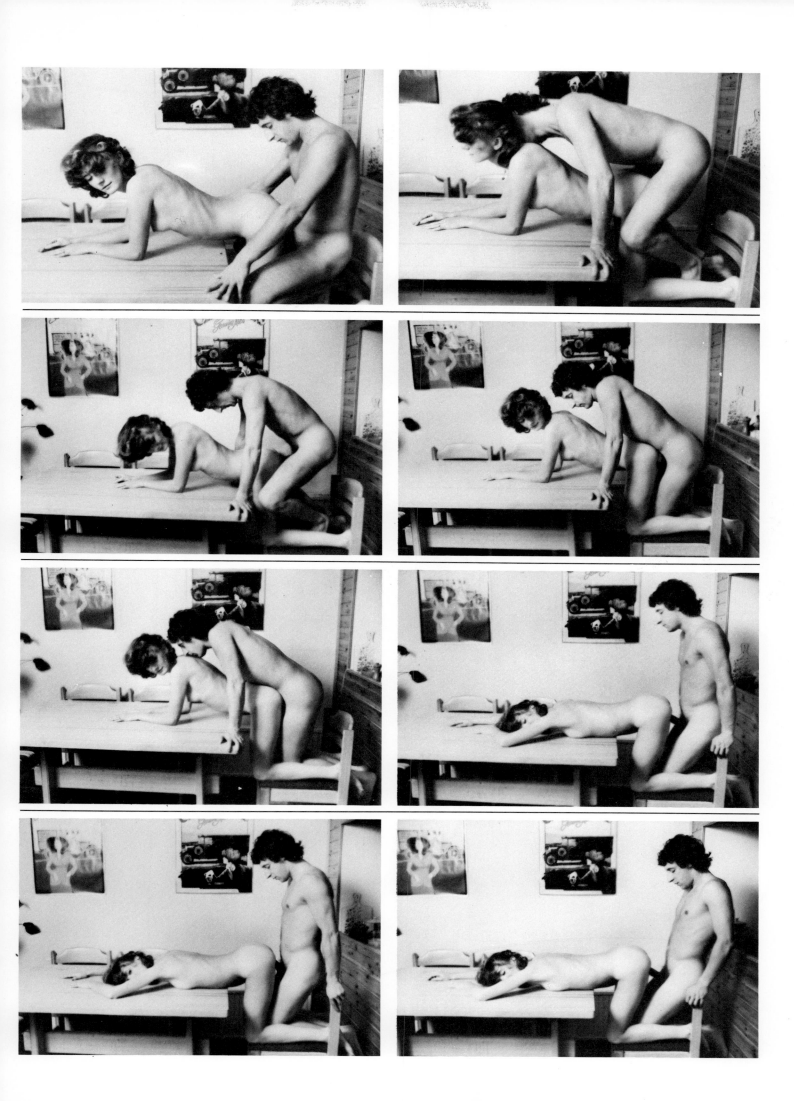

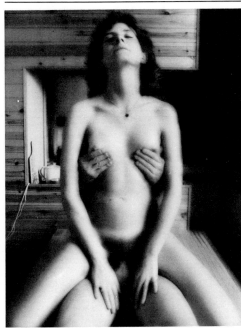

VI: FUN
& GAMES

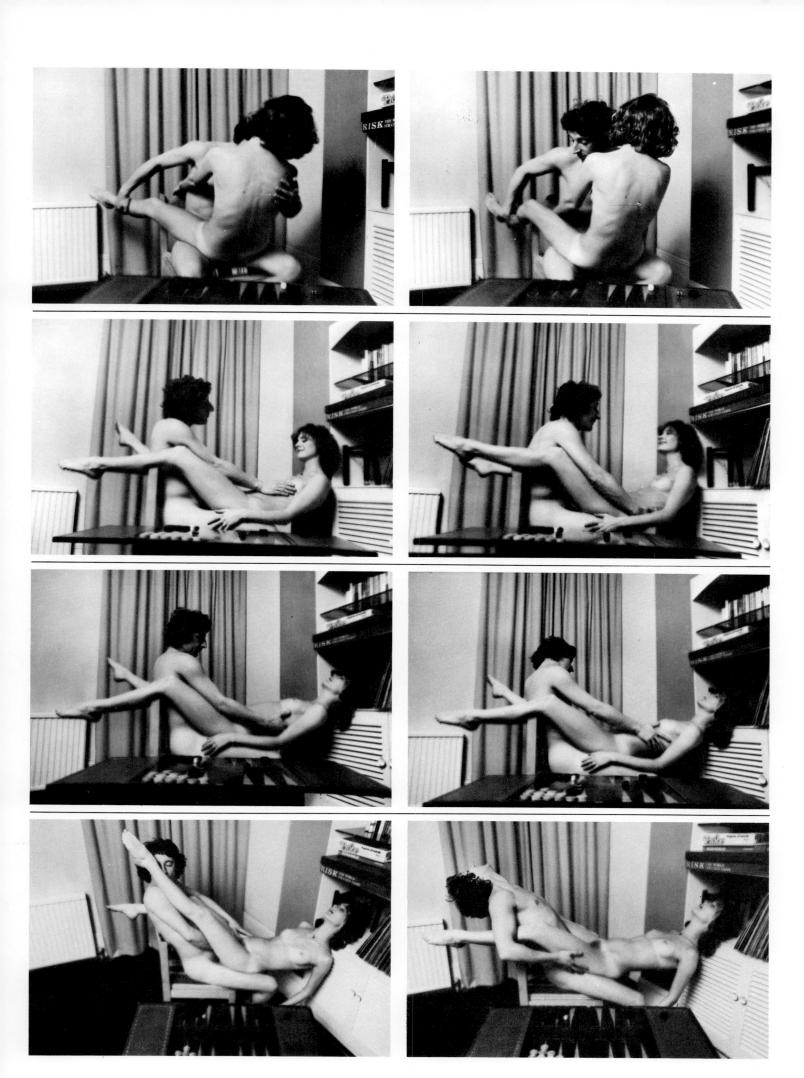

 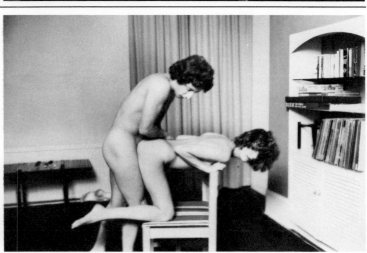

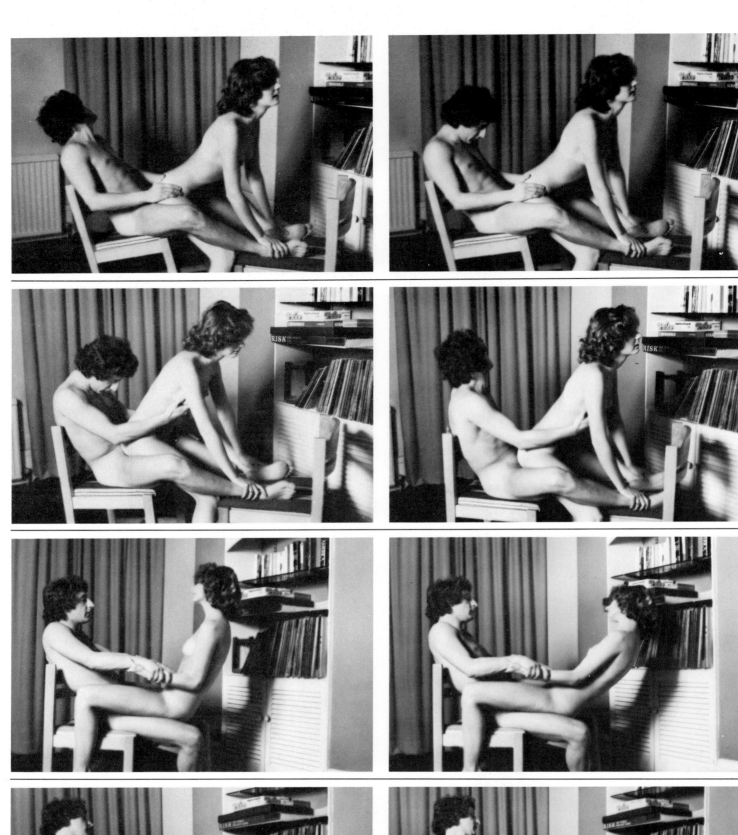
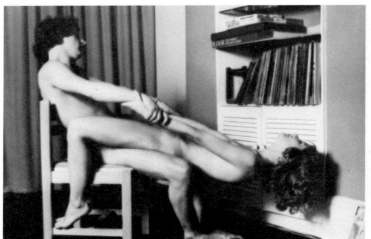

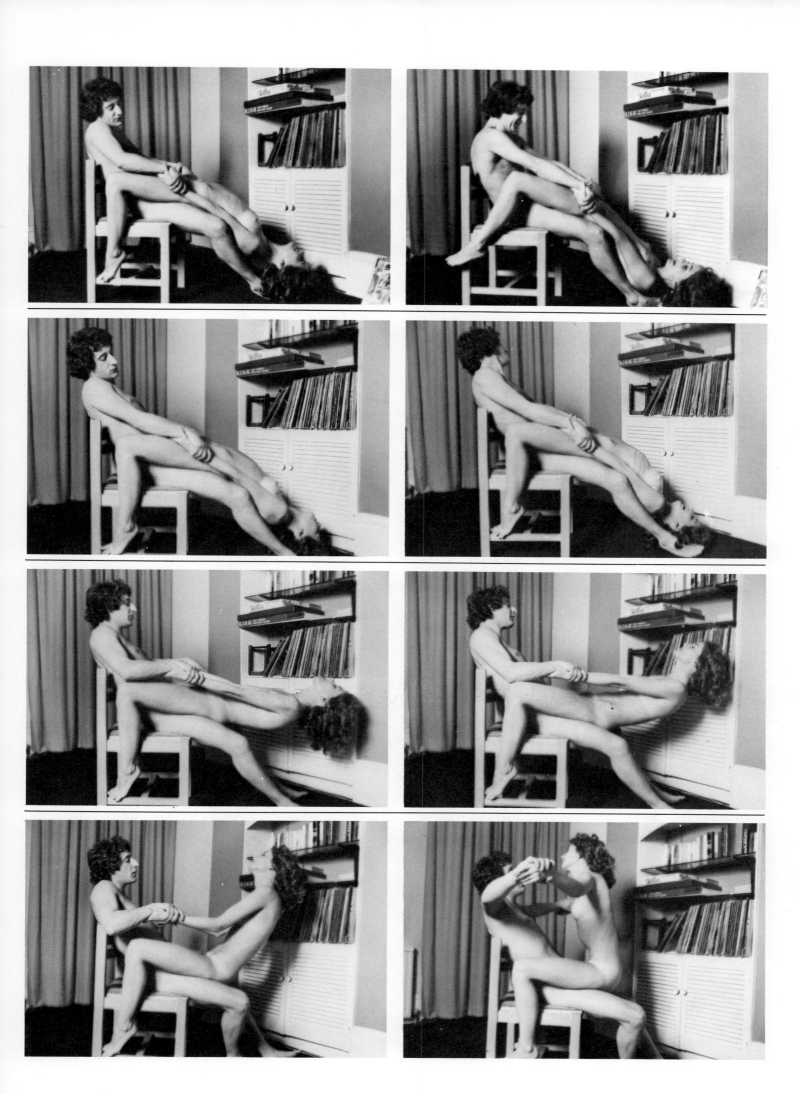

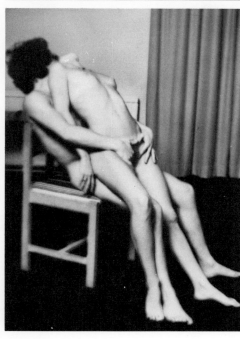

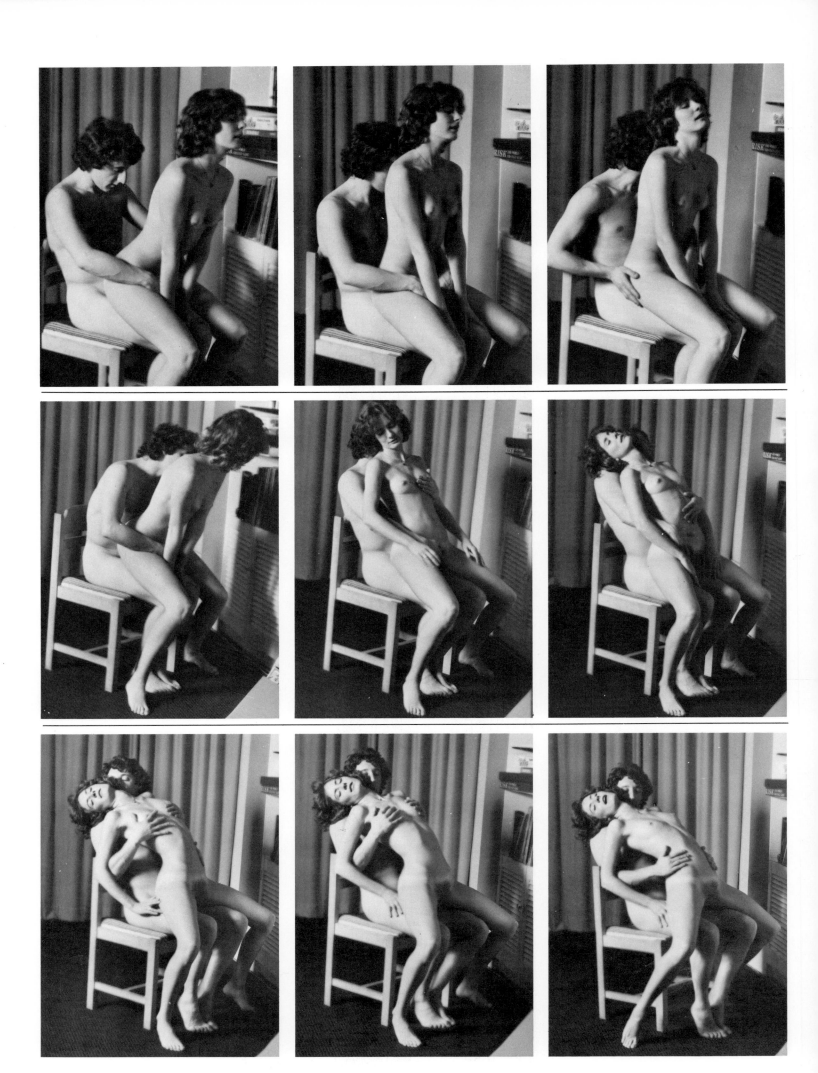

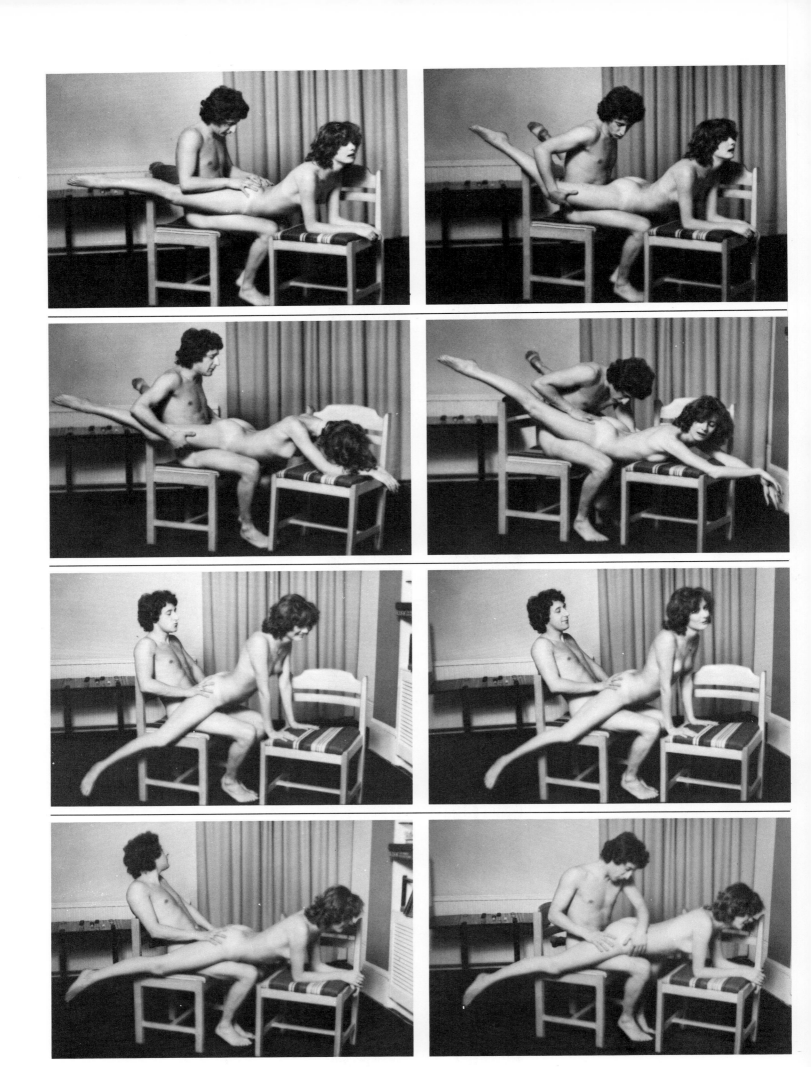

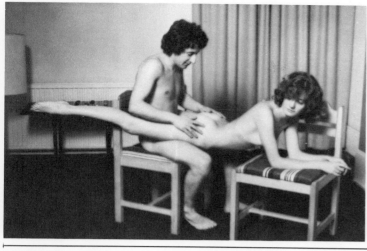

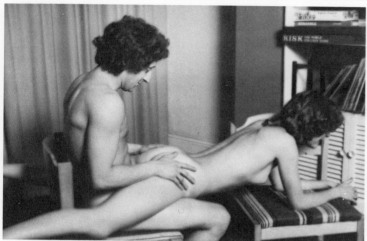
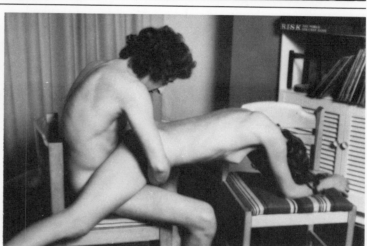

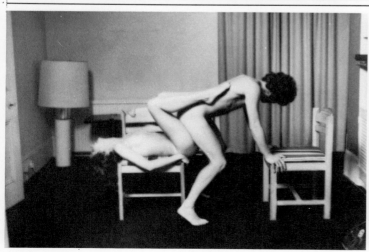
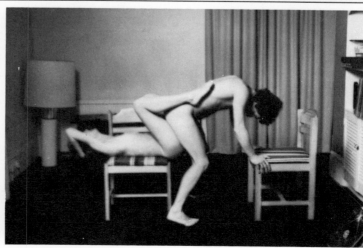

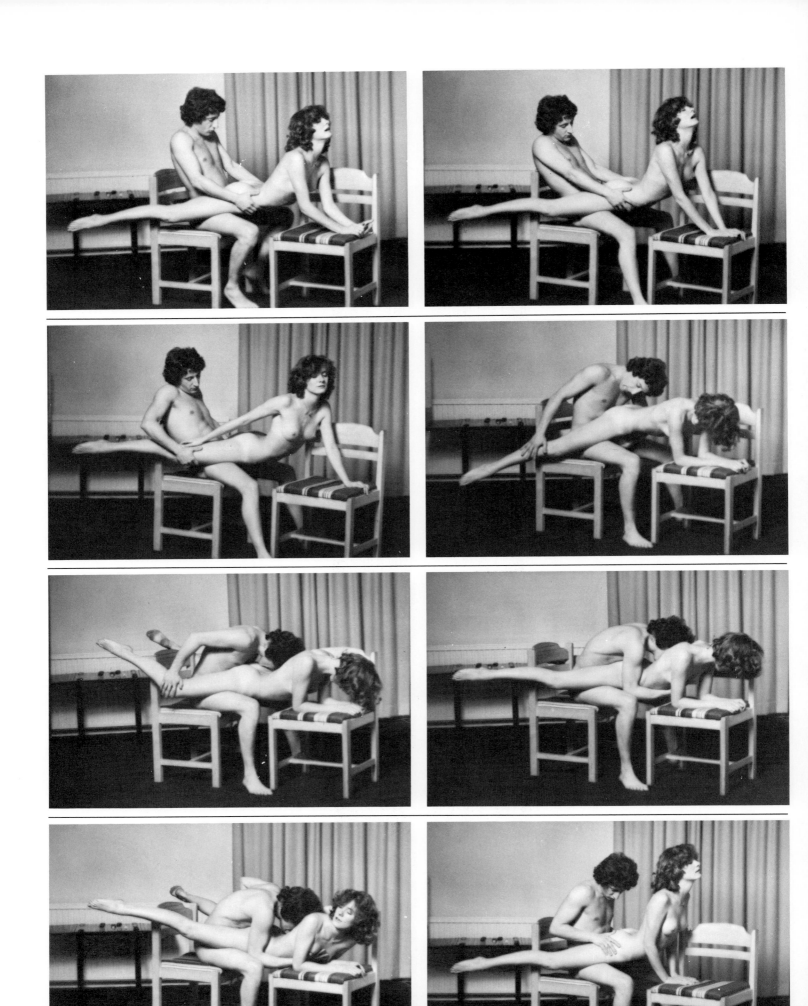

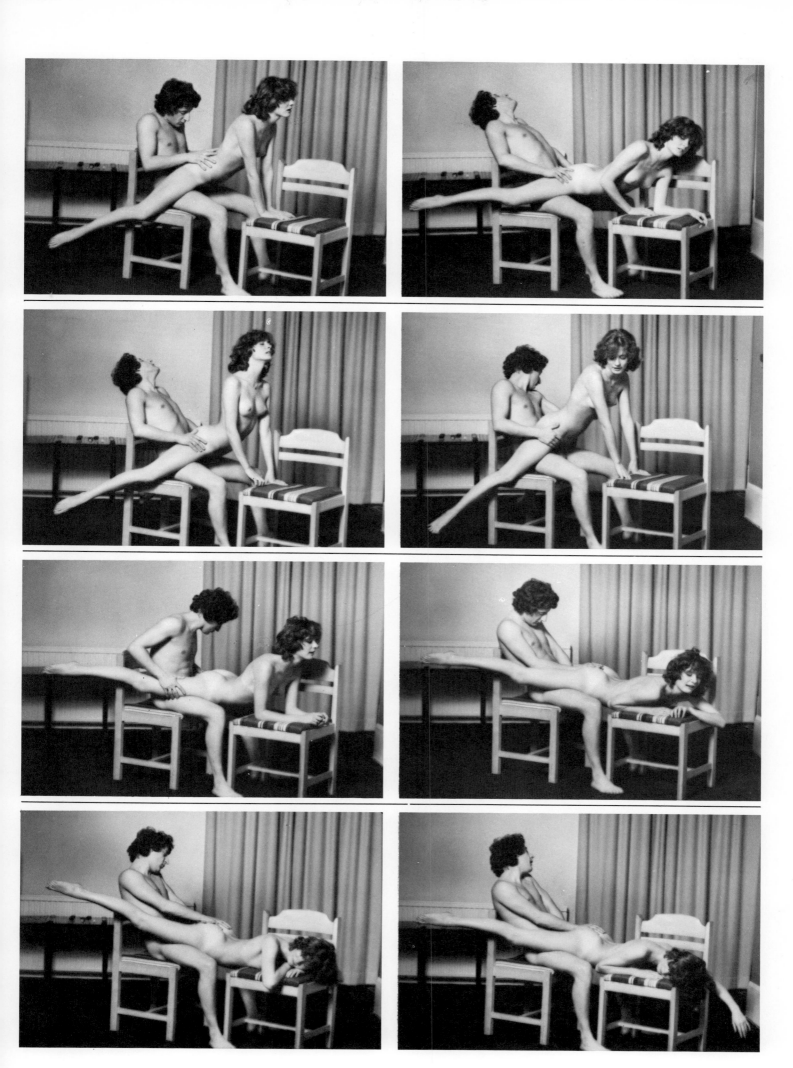

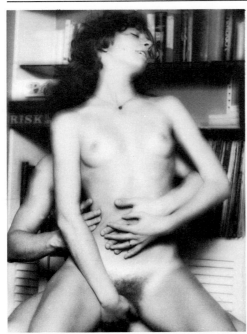

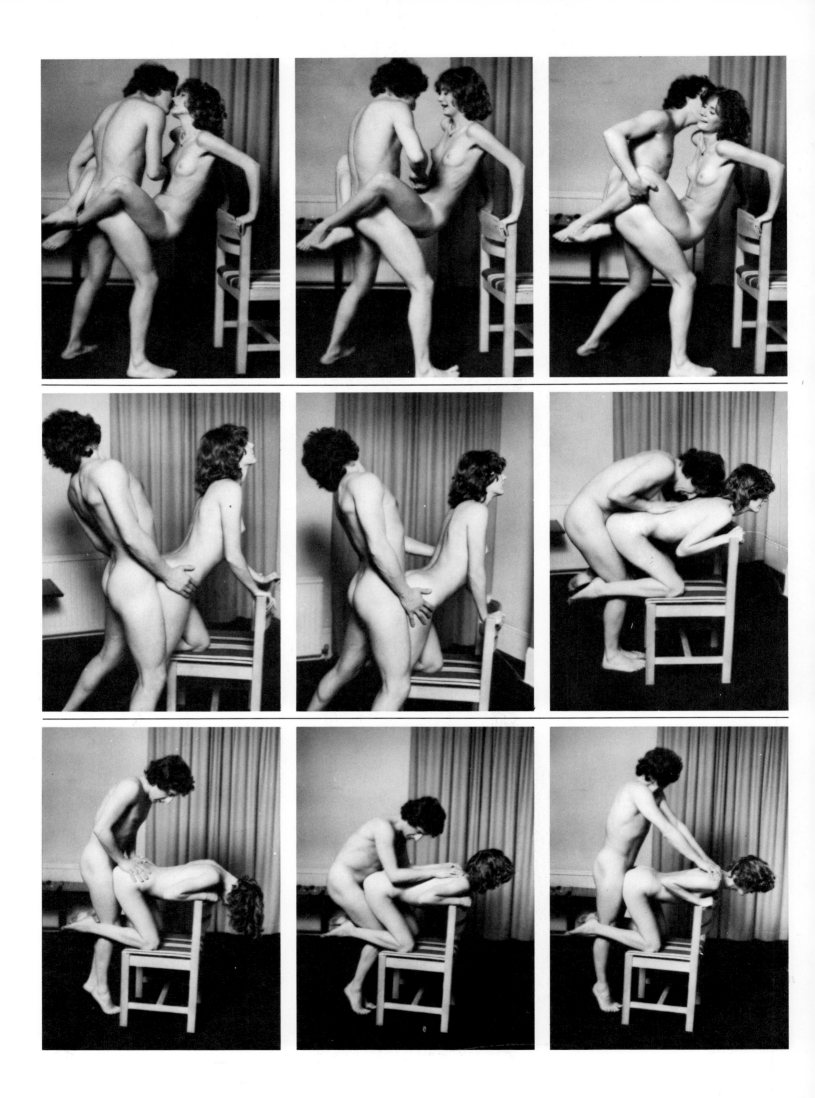

 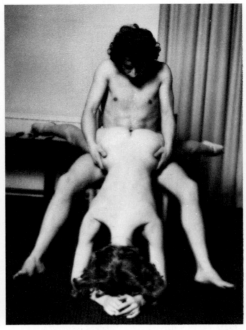 

VII: CUPID'S COUCH

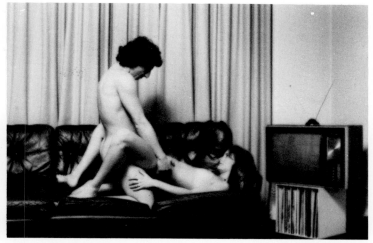

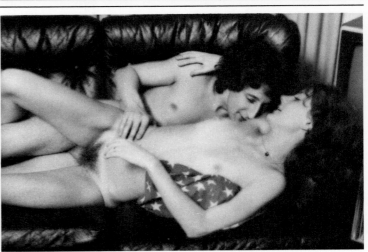

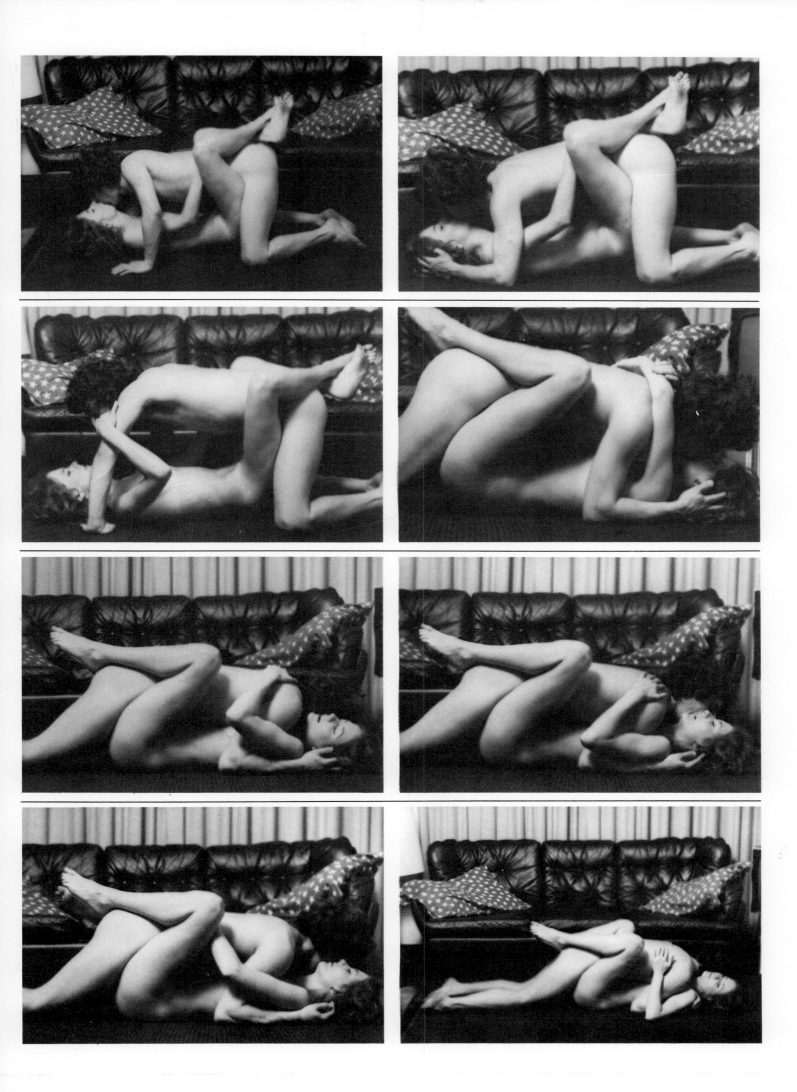

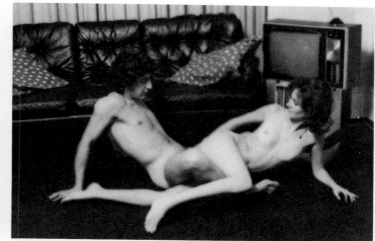

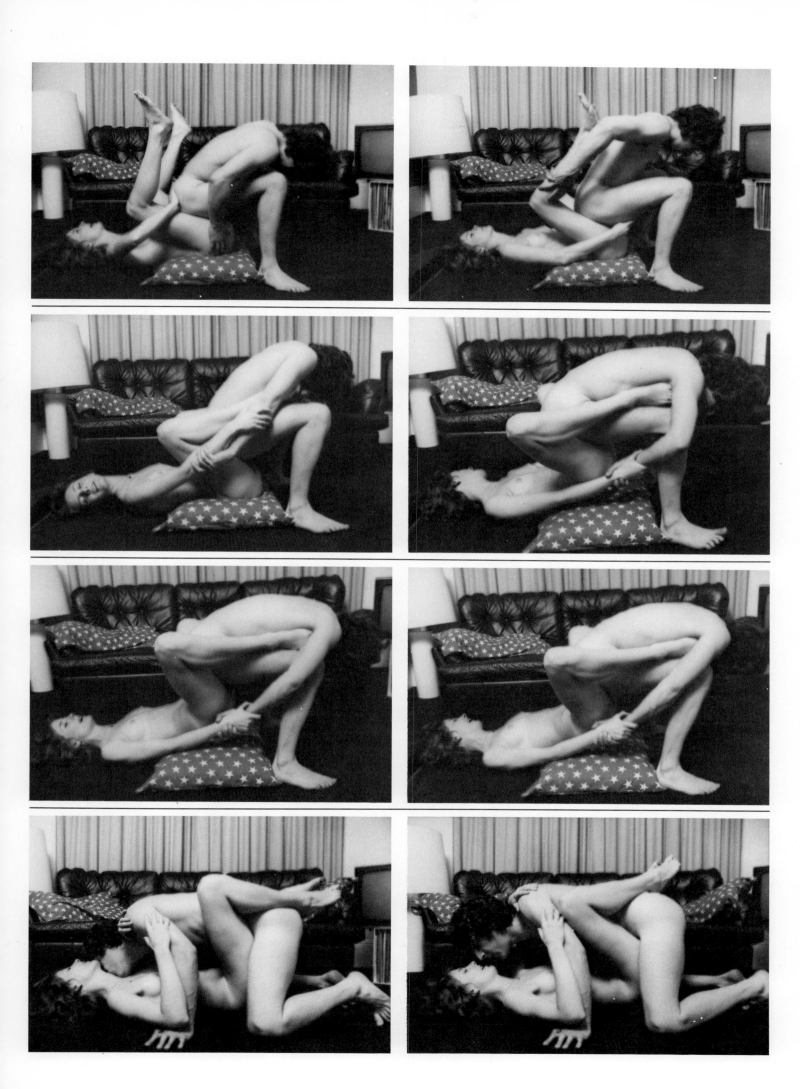

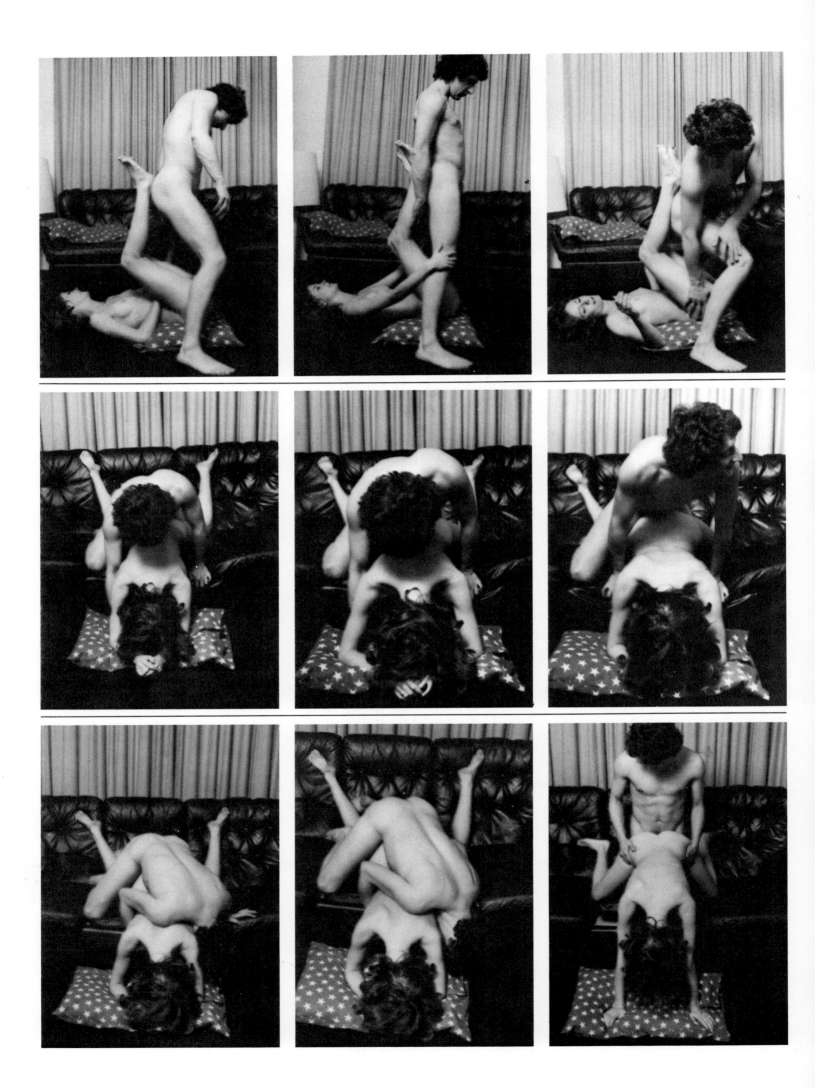

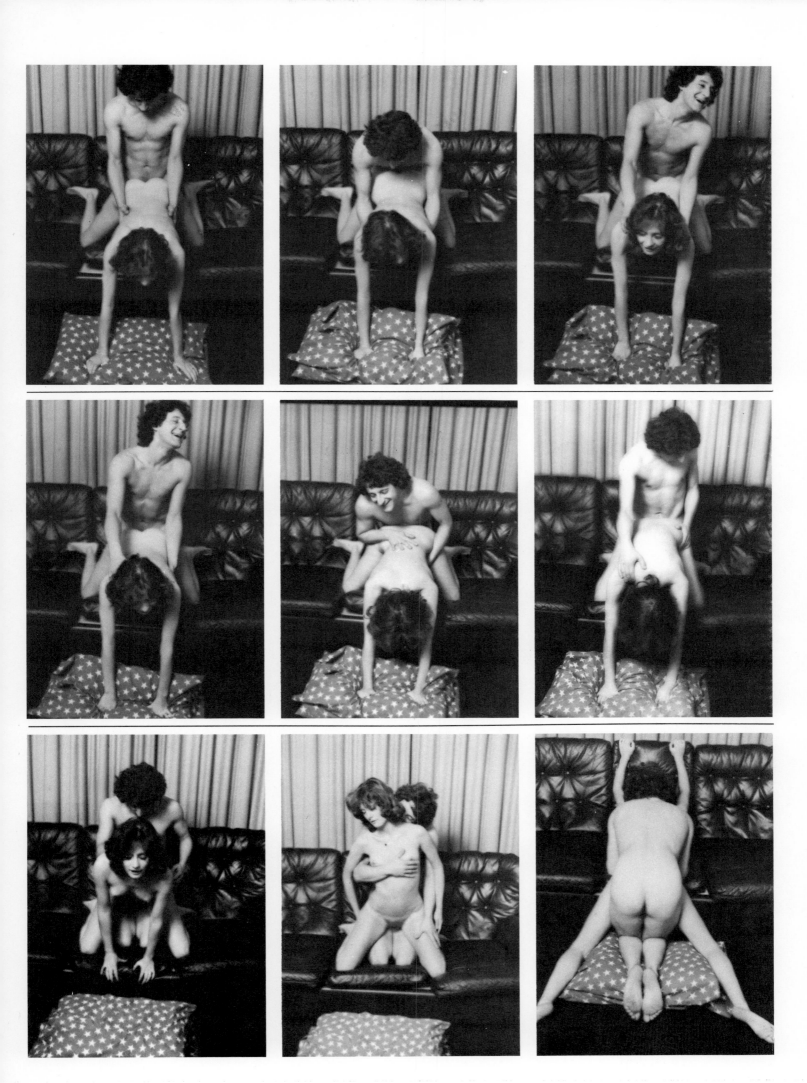

VIII: PLAYING IN THE CHILDREN'S ROOM

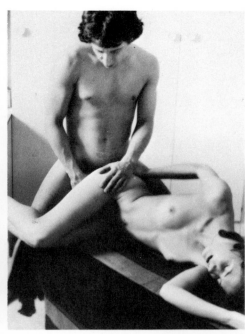
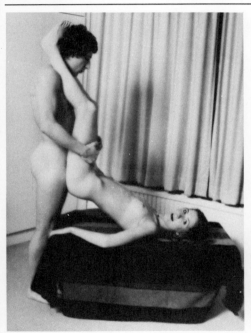
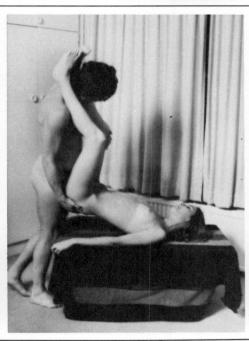
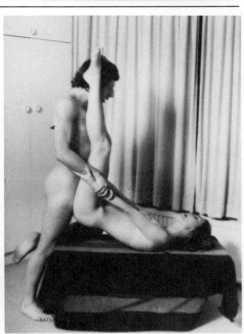

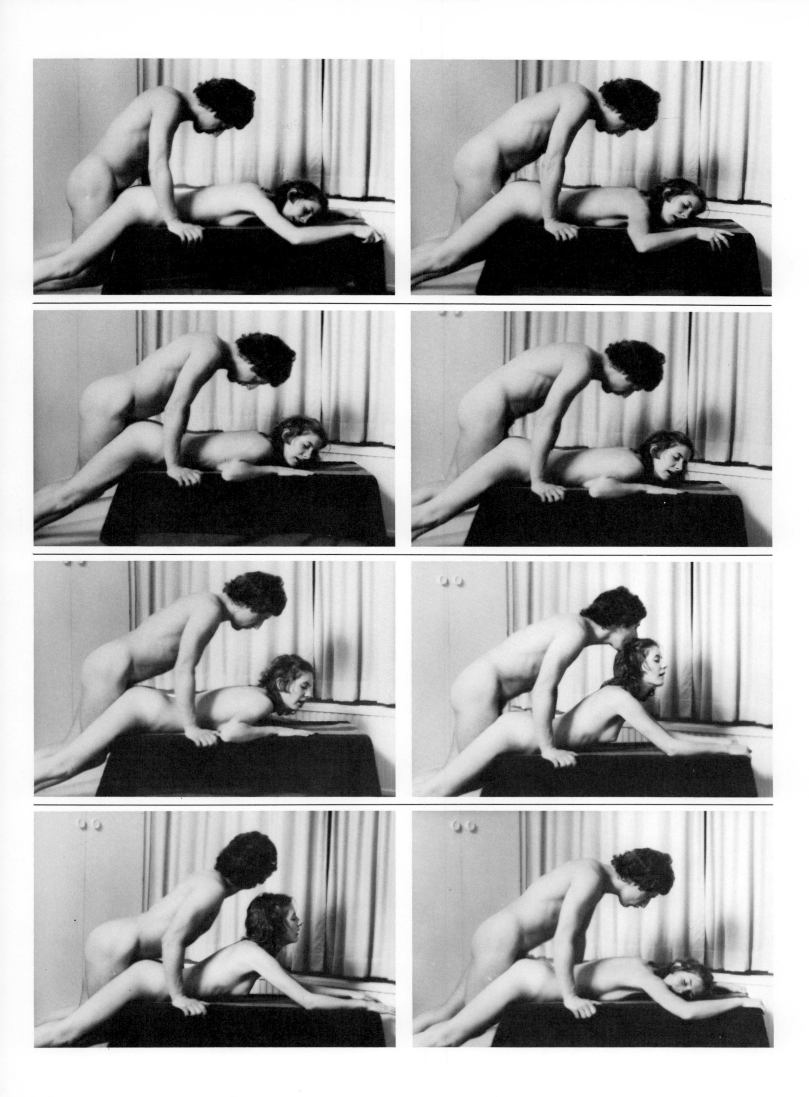

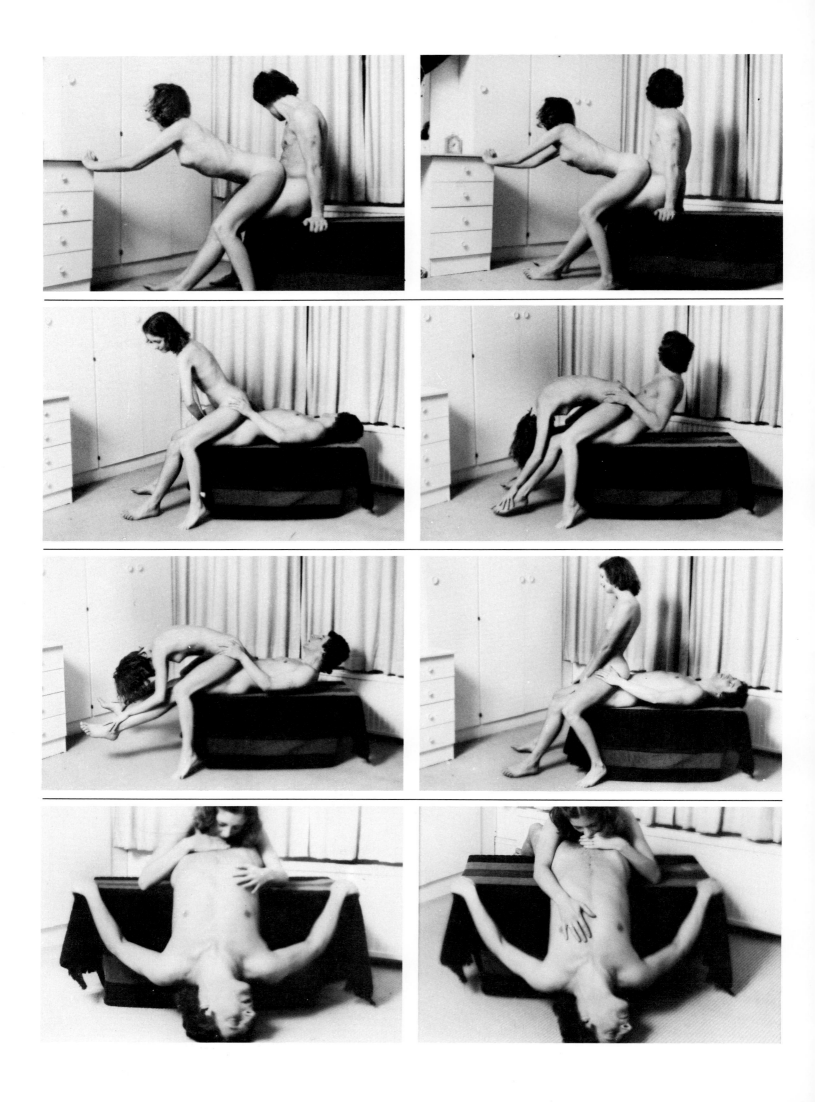

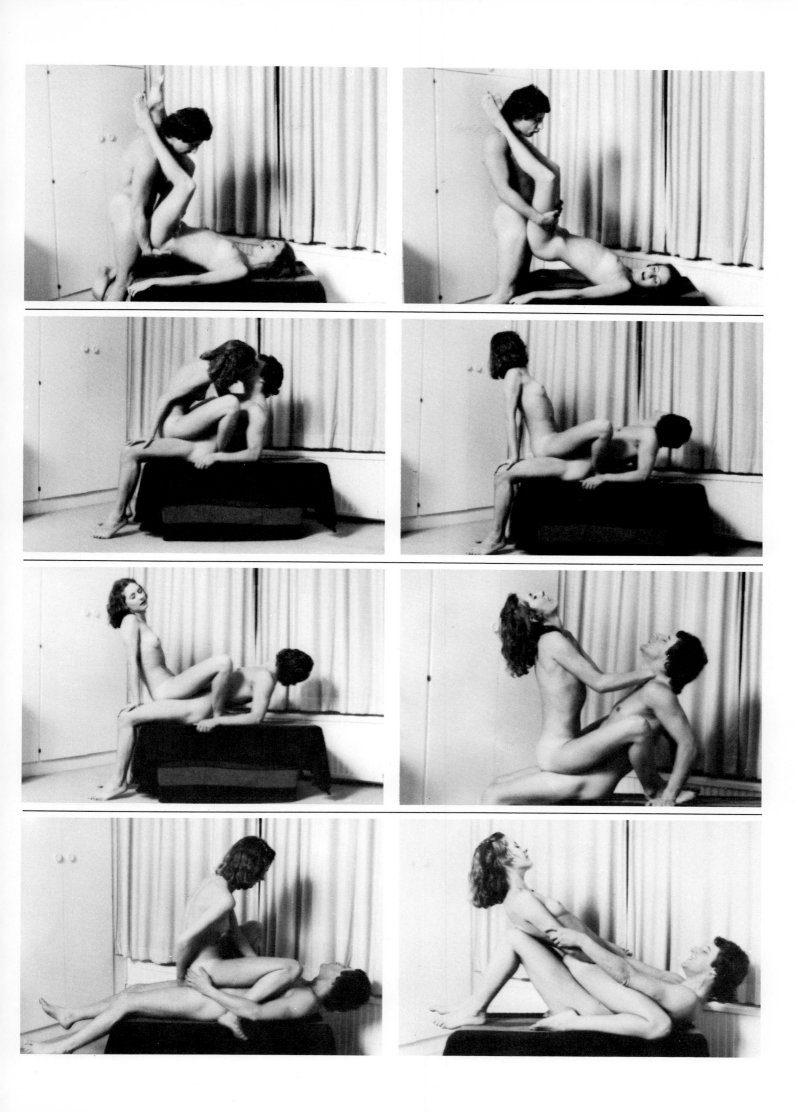

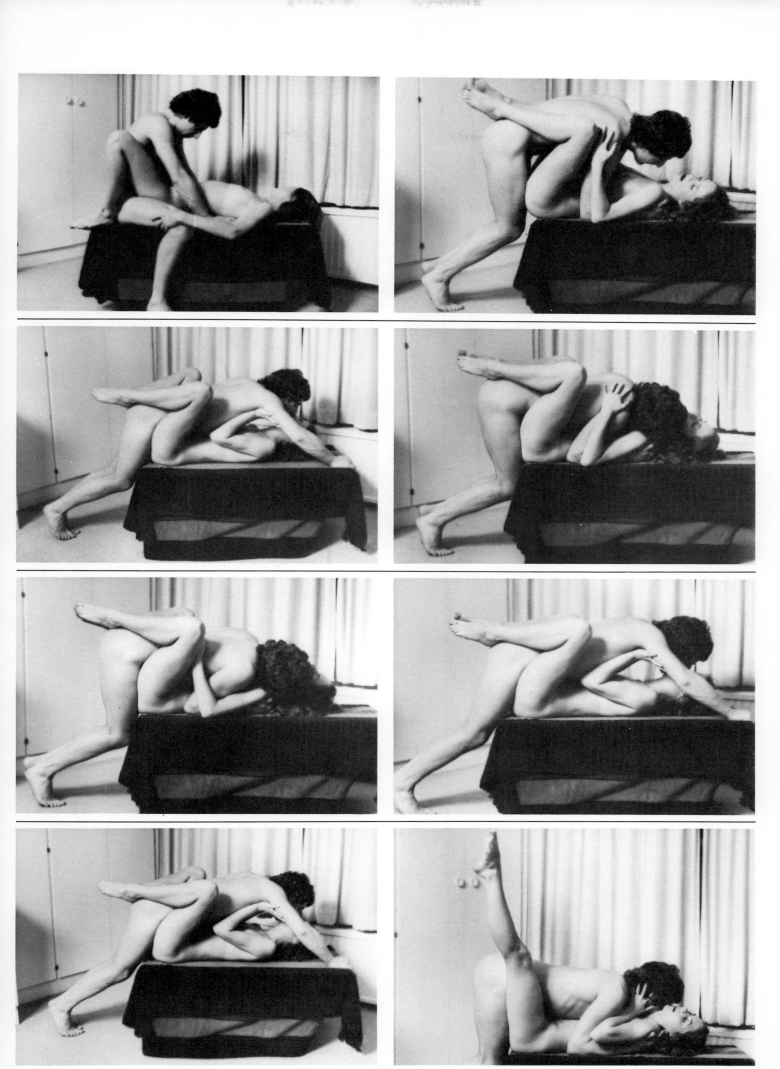

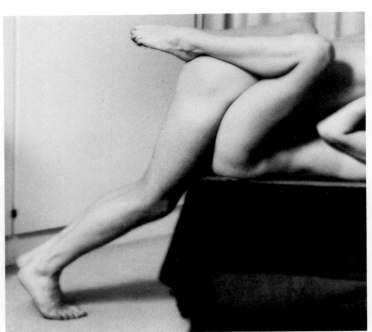

IX: TO-GETHER-NESS

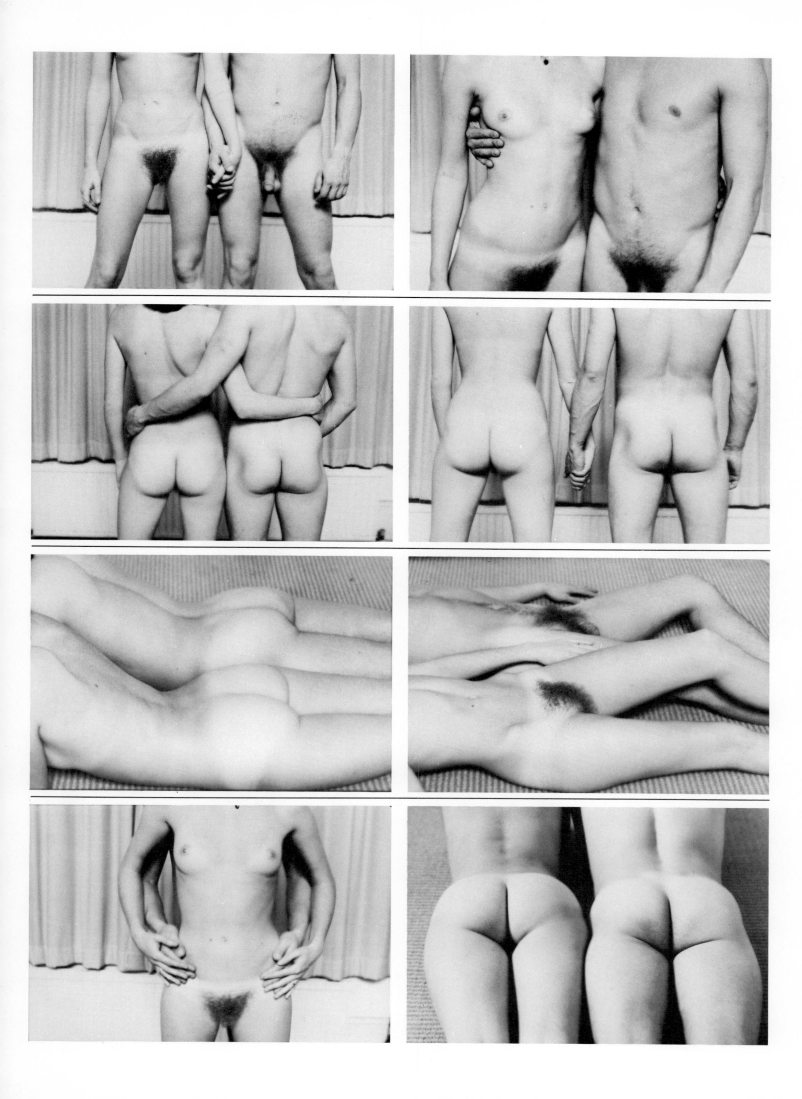

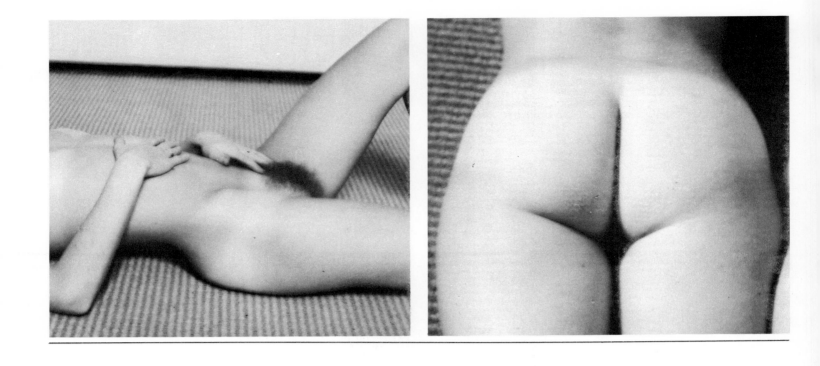

X: AND
SO TO BED

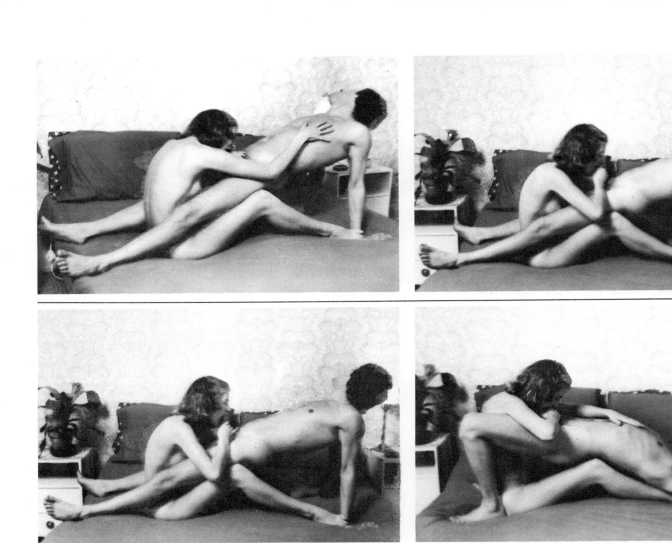

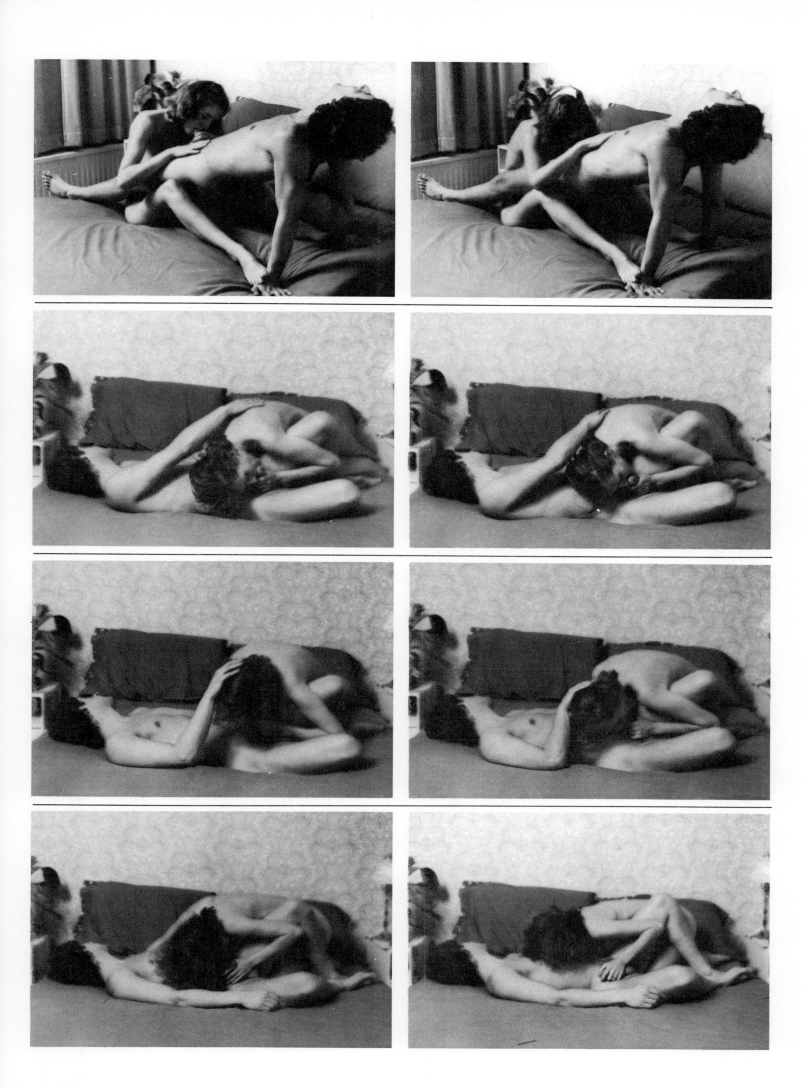

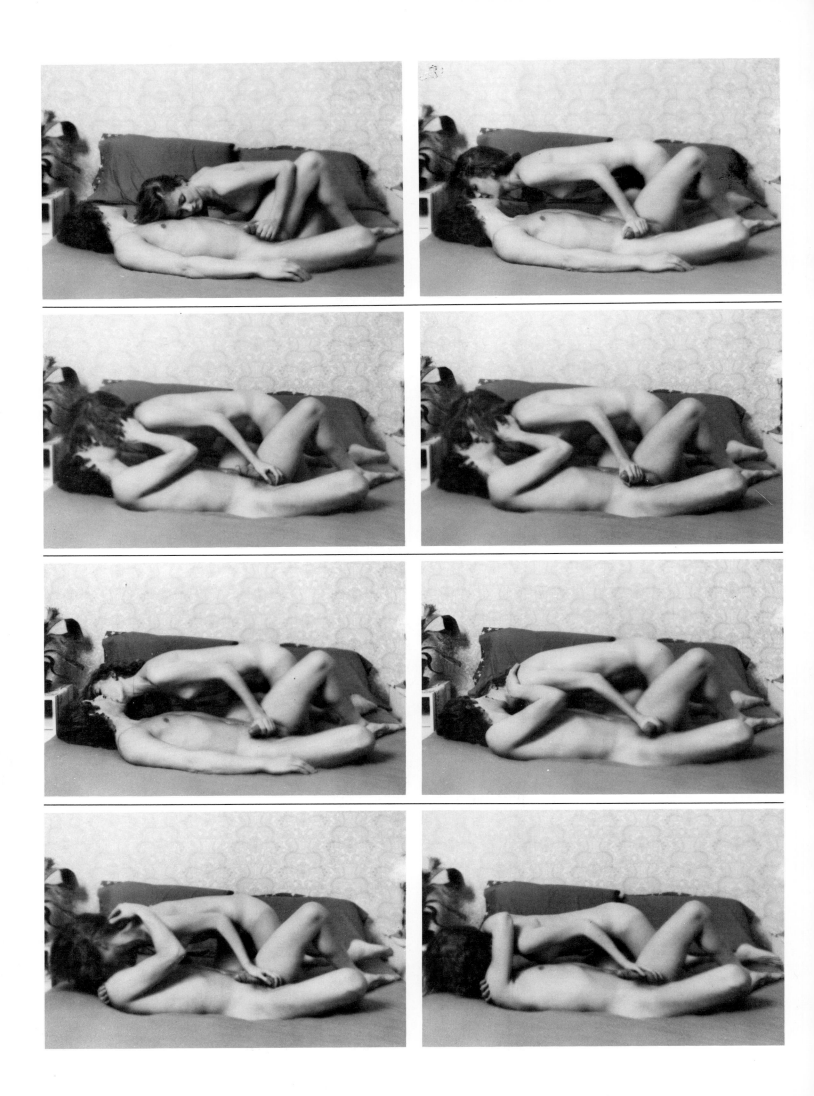

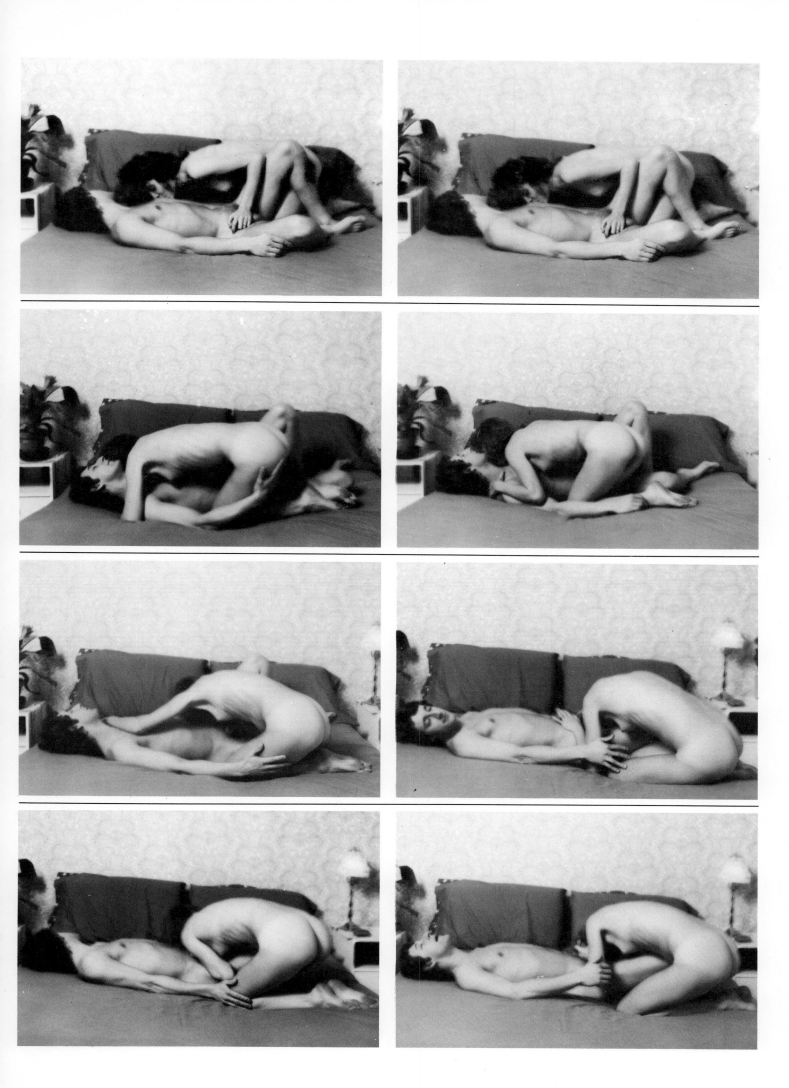

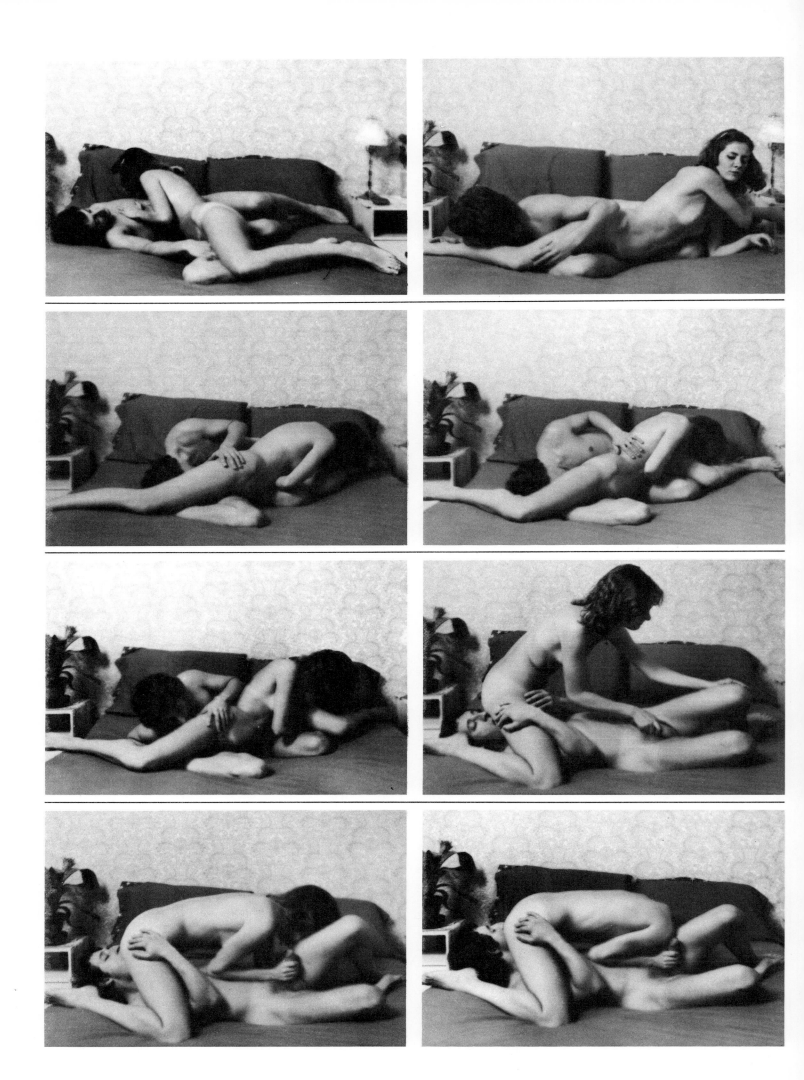

  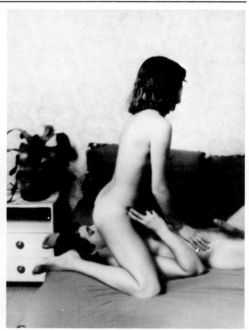

  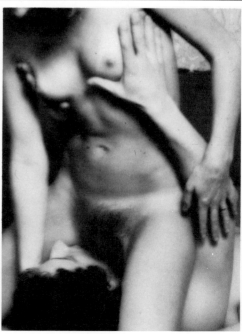

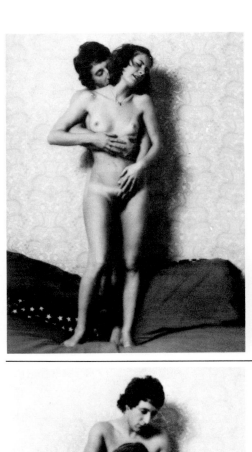

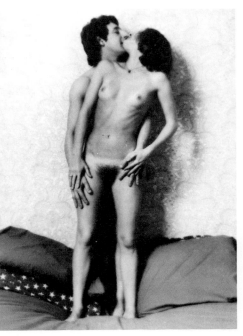

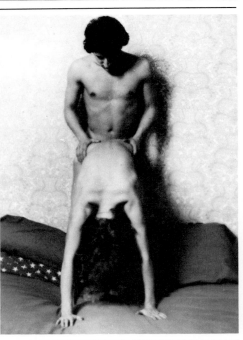

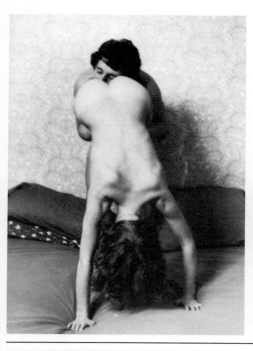  

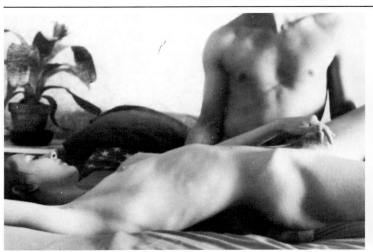

XI: GOOD MORNING

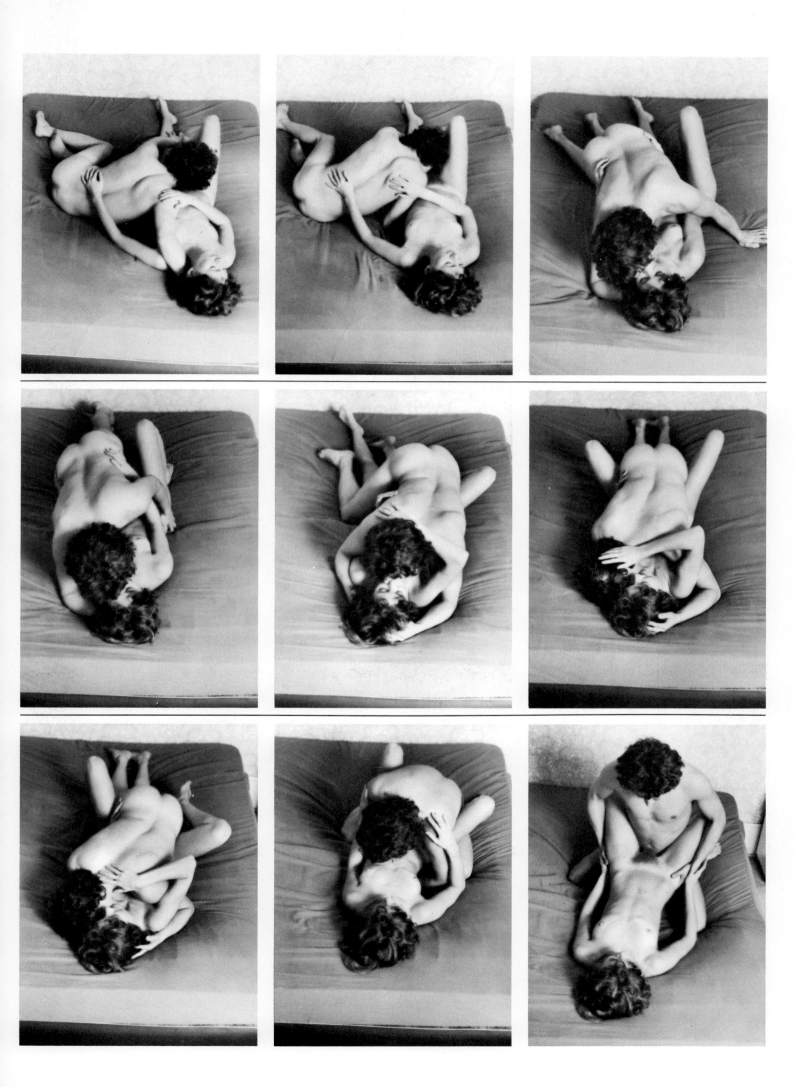

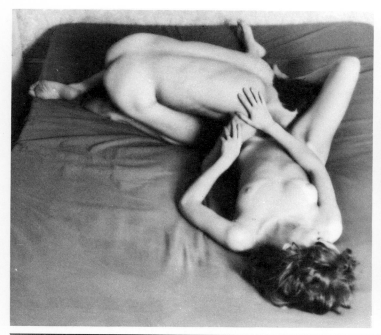

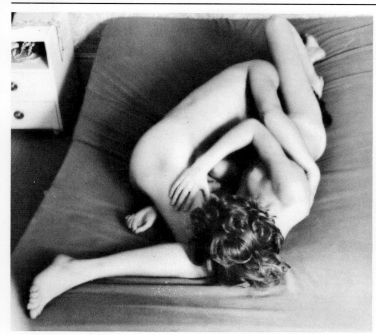

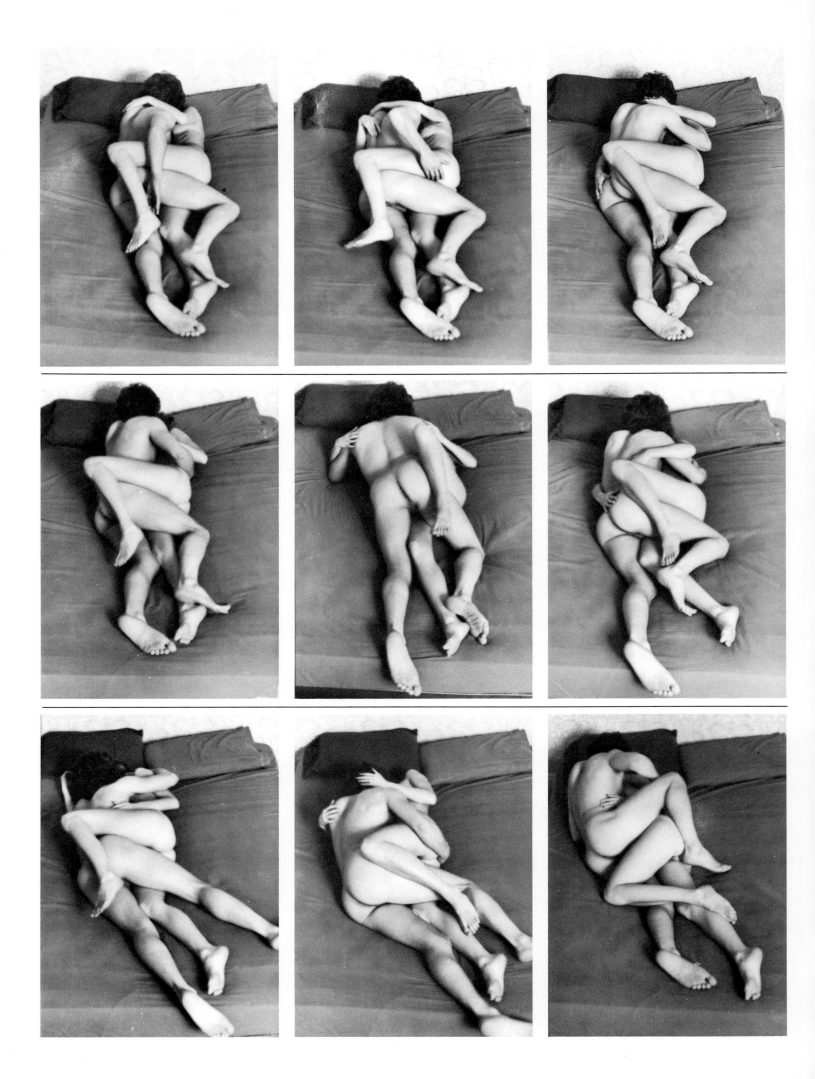

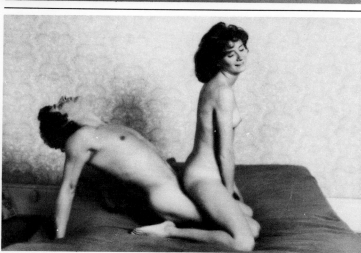

XII: GOOD CLEAN FUN

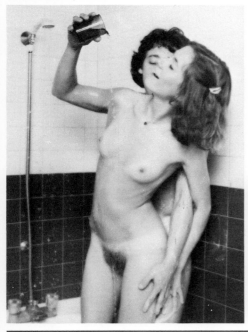

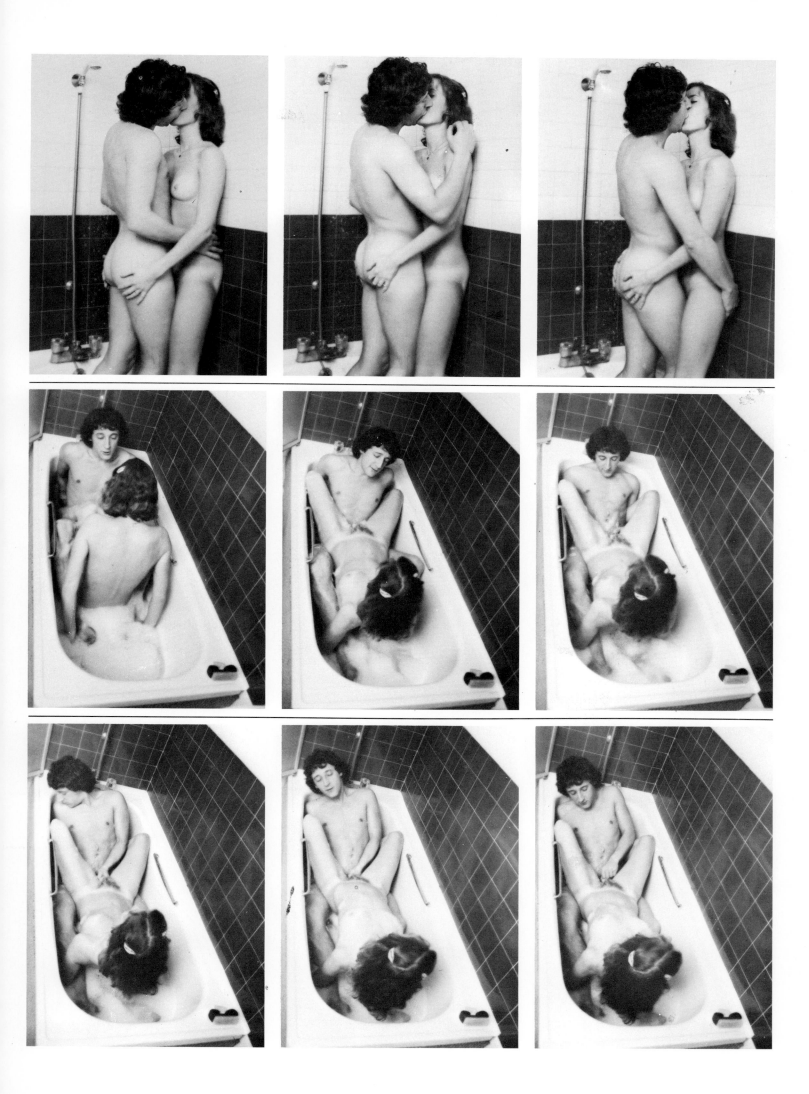

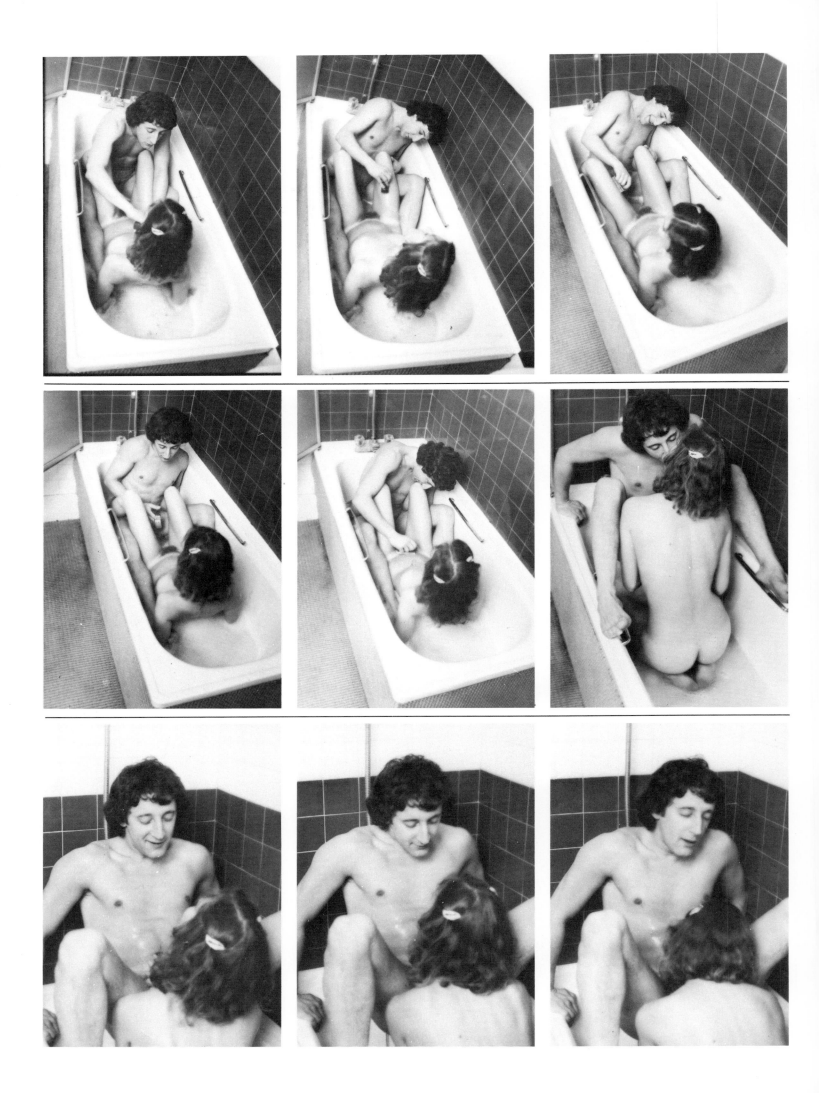

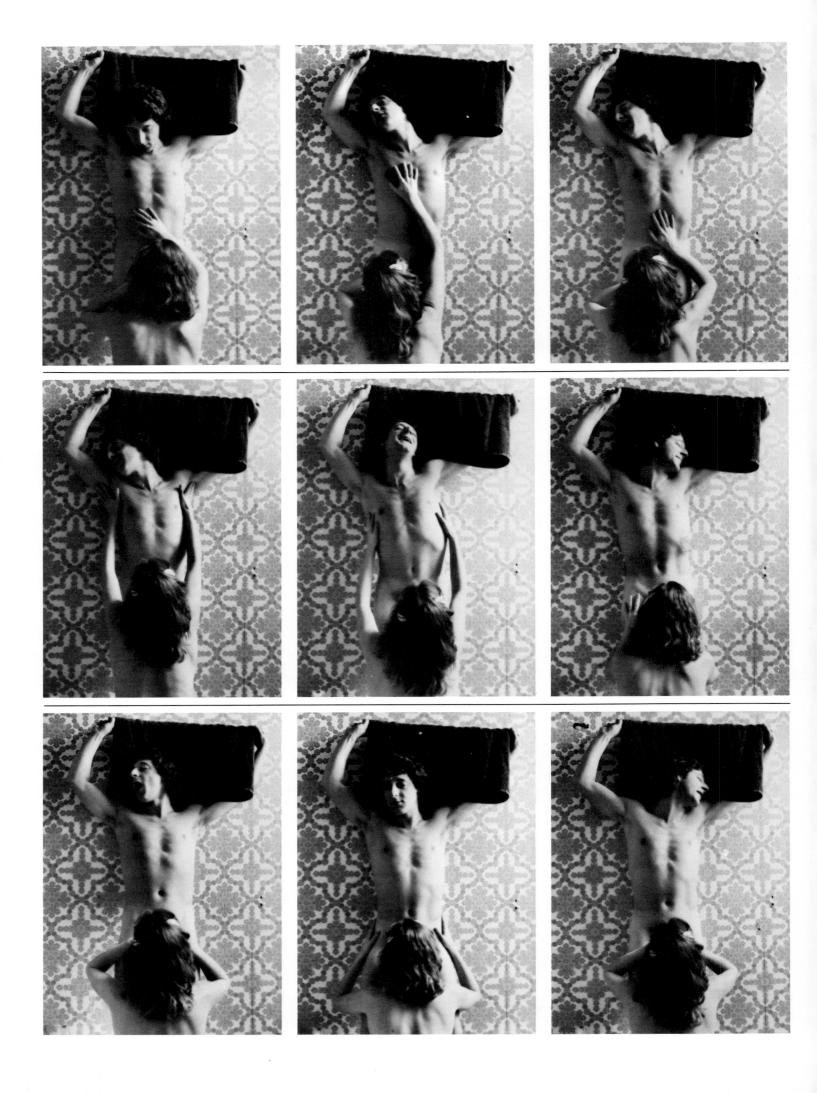

XIII: WHAT A WEEKEND!

MARRIAGE IS THE MOST